PATH OF THE ANGELS

Twelve Adventure Stories in the Series TRACKING WITH ANGELS

Barton R Thom

Cover painting by Judith A Lightfeather

Cover design by IDrewDesign

Interior design by Wynnpix Productions

Dedicated to
GOD,

My Guardian Angel Dancing Hawk,
And
My daughter
Who actually tracked the trail in
Path of the Angels

I want to thank my daughter for
every day that we spent tracking
together with Dan Wilde. I cherish
every memory.

Books by Barton R Thom in the series
TRACKING WITH ANGELS

TABLE OF CONTENTS

Introduction

In *Path of the Angels* I have opened my heart to show you, the reader, what it is like to track with and follow the *Path of the Angels*. I invite you to follow Dancing Wind and her friends, accompanied by their Guardian Angels, as they track trails of a housewife needing a miracle in her life, a teenager reacting to a thoughtless insult over her weight, a woman whose dream date turns into a nightmare, and the Angels working with Dancing Wind to fulfill the wish of a dying gold prospector made centuries earlier.

My favorite story for which I named this book is *Path of the Angels.*

"Lily had her own plans for today and they had nothing to do with looking for Spanish treasure.

"Lily (a Guardian Angel) was intent on teaching the teenaged tracker two lessons. The first lesson was to recognize a serious danger when it appeared. The second lesson was to recover a treasure far more dear and precious to Lily than a hand full of gold bars...

"The spirit would never turn and face Dancing Wind as he led her further and further away from the village. Rapidly Dancing Wind's apprehension grew more and more until she would follow the spirit no more! For Dancing Wind realized the spirit was leading her into his trap! Promptly Dancing Wind stopped following the Spirit and she told him in a loud clear and commanding voice: 'I WILL NOT FOLLOW YOU

ANOTHER STEP UNLESS YOU TURN AROUND AND
FACE ME SO I CAN SEE YOU CLEARLY. THEN TELL ME
ALL YOUR NAMES!'

"Lily knew that Dancing Wind wanted to see the
spirit's face to see if she recognized him. By looking
into his face she not only expected to see if he was an
honest man or an evil spirit but she also wanted to see
his aura, the light around his body, to help her tell if
he was telling her a lie. By insisting he tell her all his
names, she was not allowing him to tell her one alias
she would not recognize, but she was requiring him to
tell her every name he was known by, as there might
only be one of his names she recognized. The spirit of
the man refused to turn around and face her so that
Dancing Wind could clearly see his hands and face.
With his back turned towards her, he angrily told her,
'YOU NEVER TRUSTED ME.'

"Dancing Wind felt the danger this spirit
represented, so she angrily replied: 'IT IS WITH DAMN
GOOD REASON I NEVER TRUSTED YOU!' Then Dancing
Wind told him: 'NOW TURN AROUND AND FACE ME SO
I CAN SEE ALL OF YOU CLEARLY AND TELL ME ALL OF
YOUR NAMES!' But this the treacherous spirit would
not do ...."

Angels are like the trackers in this story
They follow a circular trail
They accompany you from heaven
They guide you along life's path
And when it is time they accompany you back home
They are truly your best friend
You personally selected your best friend in heaven
To accompany you on this journey
And you selected the lessons
You choose to experience and learn
So smile and enjoy life, you chose to come here
As you have before, and you will again!
For you travel the trackers trail, a circular path!

Journey to Bayonne, France

Bayonne is a beautiful city in the southwestern corner of France on the Adour and Nieve Rivers beside the Atlantic Ocean. Bayonne had three main attractions Dan was planning on showing Dancing Wind, Jardin Botanique de Bayonne (botanical gardens), Musée Bonnat (art museum) and the Musée Basque (agriculture, seafaring, and handcrafts). Yet the real purpose of their trip to France was to carry out the wishes of Antonio Domingo de Archibeque who was murdered in 1770. He had been murdered three centuries earlier (and was now a ghost or a spirit) yet he had come and spoken to Dancing Wind and requested she return to his father's place of birth to make a donation to an orphanage his dad had spoken of in his youth.

Though Antonio was dead, he had invited Dan and Dancing Wind up onto the San Juan Mountains of southwestern Colorado a decade earlier. Sometimes time seems to fly and such was the case of Dan and Dancing Wind finding the time to traveling up to Ute Creek in the San Juan Mountains, to sit down and talk with Antonio Archibeque.

On Dancing Wind's first trip up to Ute creek she had brought along a green wagon which she had planned to haul her food and camping supplies up into the mountains. After pulling the heavily loaded wagon several hundred yards she realized there was just no way she would be able to pull the wagon up high into the mountains where she wanted to go.

On Dancing Wind's second trip, she parked her jeep at the north end of Union Reservoir in the US Forest service camp ground. Then she walked over to the stream she must cross to gain access to the mountains alongside Ute Creek. On this trip she had brought her backpack and she planned to backpack into the San Juan Mountains. The tiny stream she needed to cross was not the little stream she remembered from the year before which was ten feet wide and six inches deep. The stream was now roaring along with white water which would easily sweep any hiker off their feet and drown them. It was just too dangerous to attempt a crossing of the creek.

The third attempt to journey up into the mountains by the Rio Grande Pyramid began with Dancing Wind arranging to rent two horses. The owner of the horses agreed to take Dancing Wind up upon Ute Creek and drop her off and pick her up a week later. The man agreed to do this for four hundred and fifty dollars. Then, the day before he was to meet her, he offered to take Dancing Wind to several other places instead of Ute Creek.

When he asked her why she was insisting on going camping on Ute Creek Dancing Wind told him, "That is where the Angels told me to go."

Then the man who had agreed to provide the horses told Dancing Wind, "I cannot take you tomorrow as I have a horse show I need to attend."

"Well, how about next weekend?" Dancing Wind asked.

"I am busy that weekend too."

"Well, how about the weekend after?"

"I am busy that weekend, too. In fact I am busy all year."

Since Dancing Wind had already taken the time off from work, she drove up to the area around Creed, Colorado and attempted to rent horses. Everywhere she went, the places had horses. Yet none would rent to her. Finally late in the day she tried one final place. She told the owner of the ranch where she wanted to go and asked him if he would rent her horses or else drop her off their along with a pack horse of supplies and then pick her up in a week. She told the man she would give him all the money she had, which was six hundred and fifty dollars.

Ranch owner though about it a minute then told Dancing Wind, "I will not take you there for a dollar less than four thousand and five hundred dollars!"

To take Dancing Wind riding about twelve miles back into the mountains on an established riding trail, the man had demanded an impossibly large sum of money Dancing Wind simply did not have. Sadly, Dancing Wind realized she had no choice but to cancel the trip this year.

Many years had passed since the spirit of Antonio Archibeque had asked Dancing Wind for her help. As the years passed the memory faded and Antonio's request was simply forgotten due to Dancing Wind being busy with every day activities.

Then one day Dancing Wind was talking to herself saying, "I wonder where I should go tracking."

Lily, Dancing Wind's Guardian Angel, immediately spoke up. "Have you forgotten about Antonio's request for help?"

"Maybe that trail is just not for me to track. I have already gone there a number of times and it seems some obstacles always arise so I fail to get back into the mountains on Ute Creek."

Lily paused a moment to think and them she replied, "If you want to go to college you have to attend high school first. The reason you go to high school is to learn the basic skills you will need in college. In college you are just doing the same work as high school, only at a much more advanced level."

"It may be that your earlier attempts failed or were blocked as you needed more experience under your belt before you were ready for a journey up to Ute Creek and then over to France."

"Often in life one fails at one's first or second attempt to achieve a goal or accomplish a task. People say Thomas Edison made fifteen thousand attempts at building a light bulb before he succeeded using a tungsten element.'

"What I am telling you now is, you need to hang tough, you must persist if you want to accomplish what you set out to achieve. Quitting or giving up will not get you anywhere."

"There are a million people out there who will say it is impossible to track a trail a century old. Yet I know you can do it. There are a million people out there who do not take the time or make the effort to interact with their Guardian Angels. Yet I know and you know you can do it."

"I am telling you now the same thing that Dan often tells you. *"It is persistence and hanging tough that gets the job done. Quit ability never got you anywhere."* So why don't you talk to Dan and ask him to go with you up to Ute Creek. Tell him you want to go backpacking. Who knows, Paris might be nice this time of year? I am sure you will enjoy a wonderful boat ride on the river Seine. If you go at night aboard the *bateaux mouches* it is beautiful boat ride. The Eiffel

Tower is all lit up and there is a bright beacon you will see on top. Personally I really think you will enjoy the Musée Basque in Bayonne."

In the late summer of 2012, Dan and Dancing Wind drove up to Union Reservoir west of Creed, Colorado. Here at the north end of the reservoir in the USFS parking area Dancing Wind parked the jeep. They each removed their back packs out of the back of the jeep. Two hundred feet to their west they saw first the creek they would cross. About five hundred feet beyond the creek whey would enter the pine forest they would travel through. It would be a tough day hiking, all up hill. They would be hiking along a centuries old horse trail. Visible in the far distance, high above the tree line was the gray bare rocky mountain known as the Rio Grande Pyramid. It was just past this mountain, at the junction between the East and Middle forks of Ute Creek, where their destination lay.

Ten years earlier

For it was here in the tall pine forest, between the East Ute Creek and Middle Ute Creek where Antonio had instructed Dan and Dancing Wind to meet him in 2002. Antonio had told Dancing Wind: *"I do not want to talk here (out of his home ground on Ute Creek). This is where you are to meet me."* Then he placed several pictures, into Dan and Dancing Winds mind, taken from several vantage points, of a very specific location he wanted Dancing Wind to meet him. *"When you get here we will sit down and talk. We will discuss your promise to me, and your trip to France."*

⁕⁕Ten years later⁕⁕

When Dan and Dancing Wind arrived at the location Antonio had told them to meet him sundown was fast approaching. First they found a good spot to erect their camp and erected their tent. Then they dug a small hole to bury their waste. Next they gathered firewood for their camp.

Antonio stayed off in the trees watching them set up their camp. He also scouted the Ute Creek drainage to keep an eye on two other groups of treasure hunters looking for his mine. Over the years Antonio had seen hundreds of treasure hunters looking for his mine and all had failed to find it. He also knew that, years from now, out into the future, they would still be looking for it.

Dan built a small wood fire for the night. As the sun set to the west and twilight was upon them, Dancing Wind and Dan invited the spirit of Antonio to join them at their campfire. Here all three friends sat around the campfire and talked. On this first night Antonio told them about his father who was an officer in the Spanish Army exploring the San Juan Mountains in 1684. It was here on Ute Creek where he discovered one of the richest gold mines existing in what would now be the United States. His father Jean L'Archeveque discovered three gold/silver mines in the mountains by the Rio Grande Pyramid. The richest of the three mines through some times all three mines were called by the same name, *La Mina Perdida de la Ventana* (The Mine of the Pyramid and the Window). All three mines contained fabulously rich Sylvanite gold ore. The mines are so rich that a single fist full of material pulled from the ore vein will often contain a half to one troy ounce of gold.

Antonio told Dan and Dancing Wind that he had been working the mine in the fall of 1770 when they were ambushed by Ute Indians. Normally they would have had enough men to fight off the Ute's except that half their men had left in the morning for the cache down in the mountains north of Pagosa Hot Springs. With only four men at the mine they were no match for the dozen warriors which attacked them. Antonio told them when they made their dash from the mine, two men were immediately killed and died at the mine entrance while Ramon and he made a dash for it. Ramon took off running to the east towards the window by the pyramid mountain as he hoped to catch up with the men who had left hours earlier. Ramon was killed while climbing the mountain slope about 200 yards just west of the window, La Ventana.

Antonio told us he managed to catch a mule he had tethered outside the mine entrance and he rode south up the middle fork of Ute Creek and took a trail headed south. Behind him rode almost a dozen Ute warriors intent upon killing him. About fifteen kilometers or 9 miles south of the mine he was overtaken and murdered by the Ute Indians.

As Antonio spoke to us around the camp fire, he talked about the last minutes of his life, "I had a lot of time to review my life, the best times and my regrets. It was in the moments leading up to my death, that I recalled hearing my father talking about how he grew up in Bayonne and if he ever had a chance he wanted to give some money to an orphanage to help other children in France. As I fled for my life I swore if I escaped I would carry out my father's wishes. Of course when I died, I never had a chance to carry out my father's wishes."

Dan told Dancing Wind that it was this thought, which has prevented Antonio from going *home* when he died. This thought was on his mind as he died and passed into spirit.

At the time of Antonio's physical death, he had a choice to return to heaven and go *home* or to stay here on the earth as a spirit or what some call a ghost. Since Antonio's thoughts were focused on his memories of his dad and his dad's wish Antonio felt it was up to him to carry out his dad's last wish. So Antonio was focused on returning to France and carrying out his dads wishes. Now for hundreds of years Antonio has stayed up upon Ute Creek with one main desire: To make a financial contribution to the churches and children's orphanages in Bayonne, France.

Antonio is a rich man (spirit). He has more wealth than anyone can imagine. But as a spirit he is unable to spend a penny of his wealth. His mines have tons of rich ore in them. Yet Antonio is unable to utilize his wealth to achieve any task he wishes. It must be a frustrating situation to be unable to help your wife, family and to be unable to carry out your dads request to you. Antonio has been unable to travel to France and help the orphanages of his choice.

And then after three hundred years, along comes an answer to Antonio's prayers. A teenage girl like Dancing Wind arrived, who can talk to Antonio, and who is willing to work with him so that both can achieve their goals. And that is why Antonio invited Dan and Dancing Wind to come into the San Juan Mountains. For he wants their promise to him that they will take 25% of the gold he gives them and deliver it to a church and an orphanages in his father's home town.

On the second evening around the campfire Dan, Dancing Wind and Antonio sat down for some hard negotiations. For Dan has warned Dancing Wind that while he is just here as an observer she must be extremely careful of the wording of a promise. For the wording of the promise is what binds her to her agreement with Antonio. For once she gives her *word*, she must carry out her *word*. Dan warned Dancing Wind that you cannot promise to give the money to a specific church, orphanage or padre who existed or lived three centuries ago as they may not exist at the present time in France. Antonio's understanding or reference points concerning his father's place of birth are memories told to him by his father from about

1680. The churches or orphanages existing at that time may no longer be there. Certainly promising to deliver a sum of money to a specific priest who lived in 1680 would be a difficult task to fulfill in 2012.

Negotiations began with a "simple request" by Antonio. Antonio would entrust Dancing Wind with as much money as she desired. Dancing Wind had to promise Antonio that of 25% of the gold was delivered to three places. Antonio wanted 6.5% was to go to priest who had befriended his dad. 6.5% was to go to his dad's church he attended in Bayonne and 12 % of the money was to go to an orphanage by his dad's parents' house. Antonio was sure he had made Dancing Wind a very fair offer. Literally he had offered her Cart Blanch, the keys to the richest gold mine in the United States and he had offered her all the wealth she could possibly want. Antonio smiled as he knew she was sure to accept his generous offer.

Instead of an agreement as he expected, Dancing Wind first explained to Antonio she did indeed desire to work with him. Certainly the percentages you have put on the table are more than fair, they are quiet generous. Yet then she paused and continued, "I cannot promise to give it to a specific priest in case he no longer lives in Bayonne. I can promise you that if you will accompany me to Bayonne, France that I will give you two days to find the priest you want me to give the gold to. If two days is not agreeable to you then you tell me now how many days you would like to make the decision. I will give you my *word* I will live up to the letter and the spirit of our agreement we make here today."

"If you are unable to find the priest then I will go to a church in Bayonne and give it to the Church you tell me or if you do not take me to a church in two days I will pick a church in your dad's place of birth and give them the money. For the portion of the money you choose to give as a gift to the Church I will again allow you two days to select the right church for me to give the money to. If you fail to accompany me and show me the right church then I or Dan will pick a church to donate the money too in your name or your father's name which ever you prefer."

"I think your donation to an orphanage in Bayonne is wonderful. Yet I am not sure the orphanage your father knew in 1680 still exists now. If you are willing to accompany me to France and show us the orphanage of your choice we will follow your instructions and make the gift to them. Yet if you do not take us to the orphanage of your choice in two days, we will do our best to find an orphanage or school for young children and we will make the donation there."

So around the campfire Dancing Wind and Antonio de Archibeque hammered out an agreement. Certainly it was not the exact agreement Antonio had proposed, but Dancing Wind accepted the key concepts and spirit in which Antonio chose to help the poor and needy in the town his dad had grown up in the 1600's. As the fire burned low Dancing Wind turned in for the night.

Dan got out his pipe and lit it. Then he and Antonio took a walk towards the Middle Fork of Ute Creek. They sat down on some boulders and talked for a while. Under the starry night sky they talked some of the old days, they talked some of modern events. Antonio spoke of the modern bolt action rifles, and reminisced that they would have made a difference in his final fight for life. He spoke of his wife and how he missed her and he spoke of Dancing Wind. Dan told Antonio that he could take him *home* if he was ready. Antonio told Dan he would be ready soon, he just needed a little more time.

As Dan walked back to camp Antonio accompanied him. Before Dan entered the tent and crawled into his sleeping bag Antonio told Dan that tomorrow they would go get the money (Sylvanite gold ore). I will have to scout the area to also keep an eye on the other treasure hunters camped up here on Ute Creek.

In the morning, Dan and Dancing Wind cooked their breakfast over the campfire. After breakfast Antonio appeared in camp informing them that the treasure hunters were working on the west fork of Ute Creek, over near La Mina Perdida de la Ventana. So Antonio told them he would take them to another rich mine of his on the Middle Fork of Ute Creek. Here not more than a hundred yards from an empty campsite where treasure hunters had spent the night, Antonio showed Dan and Dancing Wind his rich gold mine. First he walked them around the nine Spanish markers indicating the mines location, then he showed them where they were to remove the surface cover concealing the mine.

While Antonio kept watch, Dan and Dancing Wind removed the loose scree rocks from the entrance and then half a dozen timbers concealed under scree. Entering the mine shaft about 3 yards they saw on the floor of the mine four leather bags of Sylvanite gold ore. Each bag contained about one hundred pounds of high grade gold. Reaching into the bags Dancing Wind and Dan each extracted about twenty five pounds (12 kilograms) of the gold ore. Then they turned to leave.

Standing in the entrance way Antonio said, "Are you sure you do not want more? I told you that you can take all you wish."

Dancing Wind smiled as she walked past Antonio, "We got all we want thank you."

As Dancing Wind walked by the spirit he turned to watch her walk out of his mine. Just before she left the mine she stopped and glanced about her.

Antonio immediately read the teenage girls thoughts and he immediately realized she had glanced about to see if she saw any of his books. Antonio doubled over at the waist and had to hold on to the wall to keep from rolling onto the mine floor with laughter. Antonio laughed and laughed as it was the funniest think he had witnessed in years!

For hundreds of years most of the people he encountered were looking for his gold, many were greedy and would lie, cheat and even kill to obtain his gold. He had peaked into the teenagers mind as she was leaving his mine, her thoughts were not on gold. She was glancing about as she wanted to read his journals.

The thought just cracked Antonio up and he could not stop laughing. Tears ran down his face as he laughed. Here every one he encountered wanted his gold and when he read Dancing Winds thoughts as she was surrounded with hundreds of thousands of dollars of Sylvanite gold ore, she just wanted to read his journals about his life. The teenager was glancing about looking for his journals before leaving his gold mine.

Dan followed Dancing Wind outside the mine. Then they both carefully reconcealed the mine entrance. Antonio watched them reseal the mine. As they worked he pointed here and there where he wanted them to throw more rocks. Antonio then accompanied them back to their camp.

As they walked Dan could see a series of questions on Antonio's mind so he said, "I can see you are bursting with questions, so ask them one at a time."

"Why did you leave the gold? You each could have carried a lot more than 12 kilograms of the gold ore. I though you would both take at least two leather bags of gold."

Dan replied, "If we were too greedy and tried to take everything other treasure hunters would see we are heavily loaded down and jump to the conclusion we are packing a lot of gold. Then they would try and kill us. Not everyone up here in the mountains has the dignity and honor that you possess."

"I want you to take more gold to the orphanage."

"If you still feel that way after you accompany us to Bayonne I promise you that both of us will give you our undivided attention."

"Well what about coming up for another load tomorrow?"

"We have pushed our luck already working in plain sight of another group of treasure hunter's camp. It is simply too dangerous." Dan replied.

"I will give you my *word*, if we return here again, we will call you in and you can accompany us where ever we travel and we will keep the *spirit* of the agreement we hammered out with you last night."

Returning to their camp they packed up their gear. Shortly before noon they were hiking on the trail, on the north side of Ute Creek, at the bottom of the mountain. Several hours later they reached the forest service parking area, they got back in their jeep and headed towards Creede.

It would take them three weeks to sell all the gold ore. It was four weeks later when they purchased round trip tickets to Paris, France. They would take the train from there south to Bayonne.

****

Dancing Wind listened to the stewardess explain the emergency procedures prior to take-off. In the seat beside her sat her beloved friend and teacher Dan. Dan was a Lakota Indian who taught Dancing Wind tracking. His gray hair was braided back in two pony tails, and the lines on his face showed the many seasons he had lived. Dan looked over and smiled at his student. She was a tall and thin Arapaho teenager with long black hair reaching her waist. She would be one of his last student's he taught tracking to as he was getting along in years.

Dan smiled to himself as he saw the humor in the trail Dancing Wind was tracking as the trail was coming full circle back upon itself. For the trail to Bayonne, France had begun in 1671 with the birth of Jean L' Archeveque. It was an old trail Dancing Wind was tracking. It was at a time America was a young and unexplored country. The first settlement at James Town Virginia occurred in 1606. And the Pilgrims landed at Plymouth Rock in Massachusetts 1620. It would be another hundred years before the founding of the United States in 1776.

Over three hundred years ago a young boy was traveling with La Salle to explore the New World. The French were looking for a trade route to the West Indies, spices, furs and most of all gold. Historically the expedition was considered a failure as they returned with no route to the West Indies, They found no spices, they harvested no furs, no gold was discovered and La Salle and the men loyal to him were murdered. Jean L' Archeveque ended up in Texas as one of the few survivors of the French expedition.

In 1692 Jean L' Archeveque found himself enlisted in the Spanish army coming north into New Mexico with General Diego De Vargas expedition to reconquer New Mexico. With lots of hard work, a skill for learning Spanish and Indian dialects and his skill as a soldier Jean rose in rank from a private to a captain in the Spanish army. After helping to establishing Spanish settlements throughout New Mexico, Jean led a small expedition into Colorado. Here at the headwaters of the Rio Grande they discovered Sylvanite gold (Au, Ag) Te2 up on Ute Creek. Three hundred years after his death his trail had come full circle back to the place of his birth, and there at a church by the river Adour, four Angels and Jean L' Archeveque accompanied his son Antonio *home.*

An Act of Kindness
An Act of Feeding the Poor
An Act of Helping those in Need
Are Acts which put Humanity back
into the Human Experience

An Equal Share for Everyone

After reading a story about the gold of Lost Canyon located to the West of Granite, Colorado, Molly went to Dan and asked for his help in locating the rich gold deposit. At first Dan tried to discourage Molly from looking for the lost placer gold deposit. The more Dan tried to discourage Molly the more stubborn Molly became about locating the gold.

Suddenly Dan kind of shrugged his shoulders as if accepting the fact Molly O'Brian simply would not take his hint and drop it. So Dan asked Molly, "Has Dancing Wind agreed to go with you?"

Molly replied, "I was going to run my brilliant idea by you first. With all the gold we will find, I will bet I can have a new car and you can get one too."

"My old Ford pickup truck runs just fine, and I am very happy with it, thank you though. Well I will tell you what, you run your idea by Dancing Wind and your Guardian Angel and if they both agree to the prospecting trip, then I will agree to go too. We might as well get this life lesson out of your system so I will tag along.

Next Molly approached her Guardian Angel concerning her idea of looking for placer gold in Lost Canyon Creek so she could tell Dan she had her Guardian Angels consent. Molly's Guardian Angel was named Juan de Gulero. Juan del Gulero had been a Basque sheep herder living in Spain in his previous life in the 1770's. Because he had been such a loving and gentle man whom always enjoyed helping other, after he died of old age he went *home* to heaven and while there he chose to spend some time as a Guardian Angel for Molly O' Brian as she had been his daughter in a previous life time. In that life time Molly had been Juan de Gulero's favorite daughter helping him herd sheep which was the family livelihood. In this life time Juan de Gulero would watch over Molly as her Guardian Angel.

Juan de Gulero listened to Molly's idea, then before he could say a single word, Molly said, "I knew you would understand." Before Juan de Gulero had a chance to get in a single word edgewise, Molly ran off to talk to Dancing Wind.

As Molly ran off to find Dancing Wind, Juan de Gulero just laughed as he watched Molly's receding form as she left him in the dust. Juan de Gulero just laughed and laughed as he thought back in heaven, that there was nothing as simple as being a Guardian Angel. Now, when he was filling another Angel's shoes,

Juan de Gulero realized it was a lot harder to be a Guardian Angel than he ever realized. Today was one of those days when he found out being a Guardian Angel was just as difficult as herding a flock of sheep that never listened to what he told them. Juan said, "GOD I sure am foolish as I have a lot to learn, Molly listens to me just as well as the sheep did. This job is going to be a lot harder than I ever thought it would be."

When Molly approached Dancing Wind with her idea of making their fortune in Colorado mining placer gold, Dancing Wind insisted Molly tell her the story or what she knew.

So Molly told Dancing Wind that the Lost Canyon gold mine was a rich placer gold deposit found by some prospectors about 1880 coming over the mountains west of the town of Granite, Colorado located on the Arkansas River. The men were headed for Leadville for food as winter had come to the high country and they were headed there when a member of their party panned for gold in the creek discovered a rich placer gold deposit. They panned a couple of ounces and then they really had to leave as they were out of food. When they reached Leadville they were able to buy food but a snow storm arrived and they were unable to return to the mountains until spring. When they returned in the spring they were unable to find the location of their rich placer gold deposit.

Dancing Wind turned to Molly O'Brian and replied, "Are you crazy? This trail is over a hundred and thirty years old and hundreds of men in Colorado have already looked for it and failed to find the gold deposit again. This ranks as foolish is asking me to track a trail in the Superstition Mountains looking for the Lost Dutchman Mine which hundreds of people search for every year. The only difference being it is illegal to recover any of the gold out of the Superstition Mountains and there is a Park Ranger station at the beginning of the trail watching you go in and out. Here we will probably run into the whole canyon being covered in mining claims. One cannot go in and mine gold on another man's mining claim."

Molly pleaded to Dancing Wind, "I know you are a good tracker. I have seen you track trails that were made over a century ago. I know you can do it. Please. Please do it for me."

Dancing Wind replied, "I have a bad feeling about this one. Will you just walk away from this one?"

Molly answered, "Look I know you can do this."

Dancing Wind looked up in the sky as if asking GOD, "Why me?"

Dancing Wind was silent, thinking what to say.

Molly said, "I will tell you what, if you track this trail with me I will let you pick the next four trails that we track. It does not matter if they are just spirit trails, they can be in Alaska, Cambodia or Timbuktu, whatever trails you pick I will agree to them."

Dancing Wind was silent thinking for a few minutes, and then she told Molly, "I will tell you what. I will go but there are four conditions you must agree to:

1. Dan must agree to go.
2. 25% of any recovery goes to a charity Dan or I pick.
3. Since you offered me the pick of the next four sites if I help you here, I will hold you to your word.
4. The final and most important condition of all is when Dan or I tell you, "It is time to walk." You will drop this project and walk. No arguments. If either one of us says it is time to walk away and not look back, that is the end. We all walk together. OK?"

Molly quickly agreed, but if she had been a little more observant or spoken with her own Guardian Angel and listened to his counsel she would have realized she had not picked a trail her friends or her Guardian Angel would have chosen.

A week later Dan, Dancing Wind and Molly were eating in the small diner at Granite, on the west side of the Arkansas River. Molly knew that with two trackers helping her she was sure to panning gold shortly. After lunch and a four minute drive up the hill and to the west, they drove into Lost Canyon and soon Molly was in fact panning gold in a gold pan beside Dancing Wind, as Dan stood beside the stream and gave them pointers on panning gold. In no time at all Molly had panned her first gold. As she noticed two tiny specks in her pan disappointment showed on her face.

Molly turned to her friends and said, "At this rate we will starve to death on the gold I can pan from this creek."

Dan smiled at Molly's humor about them starving to death, yet underlying her statement was some truth. Two tiny specks of gold one could barely even see were certainly not going to buy them much food.

"Molly you're doing just fine. Now here is what you need to do. Start walking up this creek and at every gravel bar in the creek, and where ever you see gravel alongside the creek you need to dig out a couple gold pans full of gravel and pan them down looking for placer gold."

"I figure you will want to take at least one pan full of gravel and pan it every hundred feet as you travel west towards those hills. Once you get in the hills you will want to be panning gravel every twenty five feet. Keep your eyes open for gravel where ever you see it in the stream as well as on any of the hills near the creek. Where ever you find gravel, even if it is fifty feet above the creek you need to be taking samples and panning it in the stream."

"I will drive up the canyon a ways and set up camp while you to pan samples." Winking at Dancing Wind, Dan added, "Here is a quart jar you can fill up if you find any nuggets."

Lily, Dancing Winds Guardian Angel told the teenagers, "I am going fishing, somebody better be catching us some supper or else we will starve to death."

As Lily started walking away carrying a fishing pole, Dan and Dancing Wind looked at her fishing pole and both doubled over and started laughing as Lily walked by them and headed up the creek towards the mountains. Both realized that Lily's fishing pole had a string and a red and white bobber, but no fishing hook was attached on the end of her line. Obviously Lily did not want to hurt the fish nor catch any.

Molly looked at her two friends laughing and said, "What is so funny?" For she initially though they were laughing at her and her two tiny specks of gold.

Dancing Wind replied, "Lily does not have a hook on her fishing pole."

After seven hours of back breaking digging, collecting samples, panning down the samples, and freezing her hands in the cold water Molly and Dancing Wind arrived in the camp Dan had set up. Molly's fingers were purple from cold, she constantly rubbed her sore back, her feet were wet from slipping in the creek as she dug and panned samples.

Dan handed Molly a cup of hot cocoa he had made for her and asked her if she needed a pain reliever for her aching back. Molly collapsed in to a chair. For a while she said nothing as she was just so exhausted for the day of prospecting.

Molly then held the cocoa cup in her hands warming her fingers. She was totally exhausted. Once Molly began drinking the hot drink, Dan then dished her out a plate of beans, hot dogs and an apple he had cut up into bit size slices, and handed it to her.

Dan also handed a cup of hot cocoa to Dancing Wind and she too accepted the plate of hot dogs and beans Dan had fixed them for dinner. After dinner both teenagers went straight to their sleeping bags in the tent. It had been a long day. Dan smoked his pipe and watched the night stars for a while and then he said his prayers and he too turned in for the night.

The next morning after breakfast while Dan, Molly and Dancing Wind broke camp and rolled up their tents and sleeping bag Lily grabbed a fishing pole and headed West up the creek towards the mountains. Dan and Dancing Wind just shook their heads and smiled as both knew Lily would never catch any fish without any hook on her fishing line and besides her fishing pole and line were invisible to everyone except to Angels, ghost and a few lucky people who can see them. As Lily walked by Dan, Dan smiled at the Guardian Angel and then winked at her, for he realized the Angel did not want to hurt any fish. Then Dan resumed loading up the camping gear into his vehicle. Dan was moving the camp and setting up a new camp further up the creek in the direction Lily had taken earlier.

Molly and Dancing Wind took their, pick, shovel and gold pans and had returned to the creek taking samples and panning for gold. They would spend the day taking hundreds of samples and panning them down for gold as they worked their way west towards the mountains.

At noon Dan arrived from camp and brought the two teenage girls a large lunch and a couple bottles of water. When he asked how their prospecting was going both teenagers just shook their head like they had simply had not found any gold worth trying to save.

Molly told Dan, "All we have found are might slim pickings. My back is hurting, and my hands are frozen from panning in this ice cold mountain stream. My arms and legs are so sore, it feels like I have already dug a ton of hard packed gravel.

Dan smiled and said, "Well this is the carefree easy life of a prospector."

Molly and Dancing Wind burst out laughing, as both teenagers thought prospecting was mighty hard work.

That night about sun down the teenagers dragged themselves into camp. Dan handed each of them a hot bowl of chili beans and rice. Both teenagers were so tired the bowls of food sat untouched for ten to fifteen minutes while they tried to relax in a chair. Then they reached for their food.

Dan could tell both teenagers were completely exhausted. As soon as the teenagers ate they crawled into their tents and collapsed on top of their sleeping bags.

Dan sat watching the campfire burn for a while said his prayers and then he turned to Lily, Dancing Winds Guardian Angel and asked, "How's the fishing?"

Lily replied, "It is coming along just fine. Why today I saw nine fish. Of course I left them in the stream so they have a chance to grown bigger."

In the morning Dan watched the movements of Molly and Dancing Wind. It was obvious they were very sore as when walking they moved like an older person in their eighties or nineties. Both teenagers were rubbing their sore back and they had trouble getting out of the chairs they ate breakfast in. After breakfast they all worked to pack up the camp which Dan would move again and set up further West. Then both teenagers headed for the stream to continue their sampling and panning their samples for gold. Lily grabbed her fishing pole with a string and a little float and headed west following the stream up into the mountains. This routine was repeated every day as the prospectors sampled the gravel for gold as they continued to move further west into the mountains. While the terrain was open at first with hardly any trees in sight, after a week they were up in the steeper mountains where the stream cut through the forest.

After fourteen days of taking samples and panning them Molly and Dancing Wind rounded a small bend in the stream and there to their surprise they saw Lily sitting on a log with her fishing pole fishing in the stream.

Molly O'Brian told the Angel, "Now I know your secret fishing hole. I see why you like this spot, it is very pretty and you can sit on the log and watch the fish in the stream. Well we won't disturb you or the fish." So the teenagers left the Angel sitting on the log fishing and they moved two hundred feet up stream before resuming their sampling.

Every evening Dan would have the camp all set up and have a hot meal for the teenagers. When he asked how their day went, the teenagers just frowned and replied we did our best, but no luck. Lily would walk back to camp with her fishing pole over her shoulder and join them at camp. When asked how the fishing was she would always happily reply that it was just fine and then she would tell them how many fish she saw that day.

On the twentieth day of prospecting upon Lost Canyon Creek neither Molly nor Dancing Wind had found a good location with rich placer gold. As they walked down the stream with their pick, shovel and gold pans they encountered two prospectors. The two prospectors told Molly and Dancing Wind that they were on their mining claim. They did not mind if they panned for gold on their claim but they were not to do any serious sluicing or gold dredging without all four partners' permission. Then the two men left them and headed east walking down alongside the stream headed back towards their camp.

As Molly and Dancing Wind arrived where Lily always fished in the stream, Dancing Wind had a hunch and dug some gravel from under the log where her Guardian Angel Lily always sat. Dancing Wind could not believe her eyes when she panned down the gravel in her gold pan and there in front of her in the bottom of her gold pan were three large flakes of gold the size of water melon seeds. Dancing Wind put her finger up to her lips indicating that Molly needed to keep silent. Then Dancing Wind showed Molly the three course flakes of gold in the bottom of her gold pan. Digging down deeper in the bottom of Dancing Winds hole, Molly filled her gold pan with gravel. Once she panned down her pan full of gravel, it was all Molly could do to control her excitement as her gold pan held five large flakes of placer gold the size of water melon seeds.

Dancing Wind stepped out into the stream and, taking four shovels full of gravel, she used the gravel to fill in the hole that Molly and she had made so no trace of the hole they had dug remained. Then the teenagers walked down the stream to the east to find Dan and tell them what they had found.

Dan was back at the camp when they arrived, he was busy talking to the four men who said they were on their mining claim. These prospectors told Dan that they too were looking for the Lost Canyon gold and that is why they had staked this claim. Every year they came here to search for the gold. They had been searching these mountains for nine years. This year they had all chipped in together to purchase a Fisher two box metal detector to help them in their search for the placer gold. Unfortunately they found out that along the stream it was often giving them false positives that they had located gold or black sands, yet when they dug a hole they found nothing.

Dan was speaking to the men and asking them if they wanted to go in as partners working this mining claim. As Molly and Dancing Wind listened to the discussion the four men told Dan that they were open to a partnership. Then they added of course, if we find the gold first you cannot expect us to give you anything! Then Dan clarified what the men had said for Molly and Dancing Winds benefit to ensure they understood what the men meant.

"So if we are here working alongside you, and any of you four men find the gold first, we get nothing, right?"

One of the men replied, "Well you cannot expect us to give you anything if we find the gold first."

The other three men nodded their heads in agreement.

Dan then asked, "Now if we find the placer gold would you be willing to give everyone an equal share?"

The spokesmen for the men spoke up, "Of course we would be willing to give everyone an equal share then. Since there are five of us getting an equal share, that comes out to 20% for each of us."

"What about the teenage girls?"

The men laughed, "You can't be serious, they're just girls. We certainly are not going to give them anything! We are willing to give equal shares to everyone, except them. Look, you know, and I know, girls do not know anything about finding or mining gold, so you can't seriously expect us to give them anything!"

"Now if you really want to give them something, give it out of your equal share, nothing is going to go to those girls from our share. I won't give those girls a penny of ours."

****

That night there was a full moon. Dan, Molly and Dancing Wind went for a walk where they could talk in private. Dan lit his pipe and just slowly walked down the dirt road. Molly had asked for this life lesson so Dan was giving her time to think and work things through in her mine so she would understand this lesson and not have to repeat it time after time.

Molly began, "You know we found the Lost Canyon gold deposit."

Dan replied, "I knew that an excellent sampling plan, systematically carried out in a through manner, would result in the finding of the placer gold deposit. If you used gold pans or a magnetometer, I knew you could locate it if you persisted, hung tough and did not quit."

Silently they walked on lost in thought for several minutes.

Molly added, "I realize this lesson was for me, you knew, you both knew all along, that is why both of you were reluctant to come here.'

"Didn't you Dancing Wind?"

Dancing Wind was silent as she wanted Molly to thing her life lesson all the way through.

"You knew, didn't you, Dan?"

Dan just puffed on his pipe and said nothing.

"I should have seen it coming.'

"I should have known, when you made one of the conditions I had to agree to was---

"The final and most important condition of all is when Dan or I tell you, it is time to walk, you will drop this project and walk. No arguments. If either one of us says it is time to walk away and not look back, that is the end. We all walk together, OK?"

Dancing Wind replied, "I am your friend. That is why I am with you now."

"It is why I spent four back breaking weeks working beside you fourteen hours a day beside you digging gravel and panning it down looking for gold. It is why Dan is here too, that is what good friends do."

"Even though you knew those men would not treat us with dignity, honor or integrity?" Molly asked.

Dancing Wind replied, "Even though I knew those men would not be willing to treat us fairly as they would cheat us or anyone who tried to work with them."

Directing her question to Dan, Molly asked, "If they start by cheating Dancing Wind and myself out of any gold that we find; how much of the equal share or 20% of the gold would they be willing to share with you?"

Dan smiled though no one saw it in the moon light, for he realized that Molly was understanding the lesson she needed to learn. "Molly, it is your lesson so think on it a little and then you tell me how much gold they would be willing to share with me."

"Well let's see, there never was really any equal share for any of us as they immediately said even if we were working right beside them that if any of them found the gold the three of us would get nothing. Then while they were saying an equal share they immediately said that Dancing Wind and I get nothing. So if they were already failing to treat us fairly, before they even saw any gold, then I have to say that once they saw the gold that greed and dishonest would set in big time. I guess my answer is that your share Dan would be the same as ours. After they saw the gold they would only give you what they promised you over the campfire in writing. And since they put nothing in writing they never intend for you to get one cent!"

"Did I get it right?"

"You hit it right on the nail head." Dan replied

"So Molly what do you want to do?"

"I'll let you buy me a large breakfast at the Silver Dollar in Leadville after we pack up our camp early in the morning, then lets head for home."

Dan, Dancing Wind and Lily smiled, for they realized that Molly had learned the lesson she was supposed to learn and she had done it in a safe manner without getting hurt.

****

Early the next morning at day break, Dan and his tracking students packed up the gear in his old diesel pickup. Just before taking off down the dirt road towards Granite, Dancing Wind walked over to the camp of the four men. They were still asleep. Then she walked over to their camp fire and she bent over one of their black cast iron skillets and placed four items in it. Straightening up she then walked directly back to Dan's pickup and hopped in.

Turning to Dan and Molly, Dancing Wind said "Let's go."

****

Over a breakfast of pancakes, eggs and bacon at the Silver Dollar restaurant in Leadville, Dan looked at Dancing Wind, holding his hand outward with his palms up he said, "So?" and waited for an answer.

Dancing Wind replied, "I could not help myself, I was feeling cheeky. So I placed three large watermelon size gold flakes spread out in their black skillet by the campfire where they are sure to see it. Plus I added something to their skillet so that those men would absolutely know that a female placed the gold into their skillet.

"I want them to know, really know, they blew it, in the way they treated us."

Molly turned to Dan and said, "Why did they say agree to an equal share in one sentence and then in the next refuse to give Dancing Wind and myself anything at all?"

Dan replied, "That some people have not yet matured enough to realize that everyone is entitled to fair treatment. A hundred years ago in Washington, our Supreme Court said that a Native American Indian is not legally entitled to own anything; such as a house, land or money that their husbands gives them, as they have no rights as a person under the United States Constitution. It has taken a century for the law to reach a point where the highest court in the land recognizes the equal rights for Colored People, Indians, Asians and all Americans. While the courts now recognize that everyone is entitled to equal rights, many men have not yet incorporated that principal into their actions or behavior."

"It may take centuries more before most people always treat others with the same dignity, honor, integrity, peace, unity and respect that they themselves would like to be treated and how all people deserve to be treated."

"... the Lord comes again and again
In God-illuminated prophets
to light the way."—P. Yogananda

An Anomaly

January was a cold month. Often the thermometer dived below zero. The San de Cristo (Blood of Christ) Mountains were covered in a white winter blanket of snow. Up on the higher peaks the temperature dropped down at twenty five to fifty degrees below zero. For Dancing Wind to track trails in the mountains was simply out of the question. Once when she had been snow shoeing in the San Juan Mountains up above Coal Bank Pass at elevations in excess of ten thousand feet, she found it hard to track an ancient trail as all her energy and concentration was diverted into just trying to stay warm and not get lost in the deep mountain snow. Getting out of the mountains had become her first priority before all sunlight was gone as the temperature slipped from twenty five degrees below zero and began its evening decent as the sun went down.

Dancing Wind had taken forty-eight hours of instant boot warmers along for her snow shoeing adventure. Unfortunately the eight hour boot warmers were from a defective lot. What should have kept her feet warm for eight hours lasted only ten minutes at

twenty five degrees below zero. Her brand new
emergency transmitter/receiver, which she had opened
that day and installed with fresh new batteries,
performed equally poorly. While the manufacture
advertised a twenty four mile range, they failed to
transmit or receive any messages beyond six hundred
feet.

Reaching her car just after sunset she was never so
happy to finally be able to warm her bare feet over the
heater ducts in her jeep. Her fingers had been so numb
from cold that Dan had unlaced her boots and
removed them from her feet. While this was not the
last time Dancing Wind spent a winter day in the high
elevations of the San Juan's on future trips she took
tested equipment she knew would perform and she
also took several different means of ensuring she
could start a fire when needed.

One of the lessons Dancing Wind realized is she
needed to always be prepared in case she was forced to
spend the night in the mountains. A second lesson was
to test her equipment in the field prior to taking in on
the trail when tracking and the equipment really
needed to perform. A third lesson she learned is it is
difficult to track a trail when it is so bitter cold one's
major focus is simply on trying to stay warm.

So while Dancing Wind would have liked to be
tracking a trail in the San Juan's, on this cold January
day she realized a more prudent course of action was
to simply to use her computer to look at satellite

images of possible locations where she might track later this year.

Several years earlier she had seen a "Lue" treasure map. The story she was told one evening in a small town of Segundo, Colorado was that the map gave eleven locations of massive treasures of gold and silver. When the old man told the story to Dancing Wind as he spoke to her she saw pictures in her mind of the old man finding this treasure. The story teller told her that the majority of the treasures seemed to be located along 105 degrees 12.5 minutes of west Longitude.

The old man told Dancing Wind that once one understood the map, really understood the map, one could go off the map and still locate the treasure sites. The treasures were buried from approximately Salida, Colorado on down into Mexico. All the sites were an equal distance apart. Literally these treasures were buried along a line from Salida, Colorado down to the Mexican seaport of Veracruz.

One of the locations was near Black Lake, New Mexico and here it was said there was a field laid out like a checker board with a cache of gold or silver buried approximately every six feet in any direction one walked as long as one used a grid pattern. The field covered many acres. In each hole was buried either four hundred pounds of gold or four hundred pounds of silver.

As the old treasure hunter told this portion of the story, suddenly Dancing Wind saw pictures of this event in her mind. She literally saw the old man and a few close friends of his digging up the treasure and loading it into his pickup truck. Then she saw the men unloading the truck as they had loaded the truck so heavy that it could not cross a small ditch without getting stuck. After the men got the truck unstuck they then reloaded it with the half ton of gold they had to remove. Then the men drove north towards Eagles Nest as darkness ended the day.

As Dancing Wind listened spellbound to the old man telling her about the buried treasure he went on to explain how the original site had been cleaned out by approximately 1970. Yet he also told her, if she could solve the puzzle, she could travel further south and locate her own site.

While he never said this to her, she saw in her mind that the old man had seen a large bolder with some type of map or diagram on the boulder and from this map the old man had been able to solve the puzzle to the treasures location. The old man never told her much more about the story other than the general area of Eagles Nest or Black Lake, New Mexico. Had Dancing Wind had more data to go on she might have looked for the treasure. Yet wandering around trying to guess the location of a field or meadow in hundreds of square miles of mountains and forest did not seem very prudent.

Then one day, the story of the "LUE" treasure was on her mind and as the mountains were buried in snow, she thought maybe I can search them with satellite photos and narrow down a possible location.

So Dancing Wind began her search examining photo after photo for an anomaly. An anomaly is literally something out of place. You might say an anomaly is abnormal, unnatural, something that does not fit or does not belong there. In her second day of the search she was examining some photos of the mountains near Black Lake when she found it.

First she found one anomaly. Then she found four more anomalies spread out along a ridge line. Maybe it was nothing. Possibly though, she had cut the trail of the Jesuits. For now she could only record the latitude and longitude of the anomalies. When early summer comes she planned to go there and check out each anomaly and figure out why they had caught her attention.

****

Early in May, Dancing Wind was working on a project casting metal. She was casting a small golden owl about an inch and a half tall using the lost wax method of sand casting. First she drew the Owl design on a sketch book. Next she took a block of wax and drew the design on her wax block. Then using small tools she cut out the shape of the owl on the wax block. Next she mixed up plaster of paris and made several air holes reaching the wax owl. By heating the wax and the plaster of paris up in a furnace she melted the wax out of her form. Then she poured molten gold into the plaster of paris mold. When the gold cooled she removed the plaster of paris and there in her hands she now held a solid gold owl.

That night, in Dancing Wind's dream, the owl talked to her. First the owl pointed with his right wing to a small pile of three gold bars. Then the owl pointed to three silver bars. Next the owl pointed to a man dressed in black boots with a black silk shirt. Beside the man was his pickup truck. Into the truck the man loaded the three gold bars. In his hurry to drive off the man ran over the three silver bars as he had no interest in them.

Then Dancing Wind felt she was falling and she suddenly awoke in her bed. It was three in the morning. Dancing Wind got up and wrote down her dream in her dream journal. The dream was easily understood by Dancing Wind. The man in her dream represented a man. The gold represented material wealth. The silver represented spiritual wealth or spiritual truths. By the man's actions of hastily loading all the gold the man was only interested in material wealth. By driving over the silver bars the man had no interest or respect for spiritual truths. The three was giving importance to the dream as well as emphasizing three.

When Dancing Wind was down visiting Dan, she told him about her dream.

Dan told his tracking student, "Have you written the dream down in your dream journal?"

"Yes, I wrote it down that night."

"Good, now keep the dream to yourself. Yet do not forget the warning you have been given. If an owl, who represents wisdom, comes and tells you about a future event, you better take it seriously.

"Now show me the casting you made of the Owl. In the future you will be making more castings of animals such as turtles and birds."

"I always delight in hearing your predictions of future events. I remember your telling me years ago about my writing of the stories of our different adventures and filling book after book."

"As you know Dan, I resisted that idea for a long time, as I thought someone else would write the stories."

"As I figure it, you have already made at least a hundred predictions of future events that have already occurred. I think about a dozen predictions you have made about me are yet to happen."

Dan smiled at his student, yet said nothing.

Dancing Wind said, "What? Tell me."

Dan replied, "I did not say anything."

Dancing Wind, "I know that look, you are seeing a future event right now as we speak.

Dan laughed. "Oh I was just thinking of Disney Land and how its creator, Walt Disney, had a wonderful imagination."

"Really?

"Yes, really. Sometimes I see a wicked sense of humor in you too you know. On some occasions you can really be cheeky, too."

Then Dan added, "Now you were going to tell me about the anomalies you found weren't you?"

"I was using satellite imaginary to look for the LUE site, along 105 degrees 12.5 minutes of longitude when I spotted five anomalies. They are on the top rim of a canyon on the east side of a north south canyon east of Black Lake. I also saw an African woman's head there too."

"So what do you figure you got?"

"Jesuits."

"Jesuits? How do six anomalies, get you from anomalies, to Jesuits?"

"The same way you can look at a church, say La Iglesa de la Conpania (Church of the Society of Jesus) down south and see the seven tons of gold in the church and then wonder where the Jesuits who build that church came up will all the gold inside her."

"Suppose the old treasure hunter who told me about the field of gold, literally spoke the truth. Then there were literally tons of gold and silver buried in that field. There were only two forces in the 1600's and 1700's who had the power and the ability to amass and control such enormous wealth. The King of Spain could and did openly have that kind of power. The Jesuits may have also welded that kind of power under the table and done so covertly. Now if it was the kings gold where would it have been stored on its way down to the seaport of Veracruz? My guess it it would be stored within a short ride of the Palace of the Governors and the Presidio of Spanish soldiers quartered in Santa Fe? Or would the King have ordered his soldiers to hide the gold in a remote location off the main trails, in a remote location where access is difficult and far away from his government officials and soldiers who were there protecting his interest.

"The King of Spain was so particular about how and where his gold was transported that there were official routes which were the only allowed roads or trails for transporting gold bullion. To leave his official route simply was not done as the penalty was death. Even today when you look at 'The Plate Fleet Collection' in Florida, you see the king's control of gold and silver by his requiring his seal on the bars of bullion and the tax stamp showing the 'Quinto' or royal fifth has been paid to the king.

"So the only ones who would have the resources, nerve and the intelligence to go up against the King of Spain would be the Jesuits. I believe they were directly or indirectly mining or looting of Aztec gold on a massive scale in North and South America. Just maybe the reason the for the Jesuit arrest and expulsion from the regions controlled by the Spanish crown was the king learned that the Jesuits were trying to avoid paying the Royal Fifth or they were trying to get the tax removed so they could then move a massive amount of gold and silver back to the Old World.

"Certainly the King's order for their arrest after midnight on June 25 & 26, 1767, and his orders for secrecy in carrying out his orders for their arrest showed he wanted the authorities to catch the Jesuits completely by surprise. The king was not overly concerned about the Jesuits welfare as he had them tortured to death in Mexico City and he also ordered the seizure of all their financial assets as well as all their property."

Dan asked, "So if you have five anomalies, I take it your theory at this point is they are large trail markers which will lead you to the cache site, am I right?"

"That's my idea" Dancing Wind replied.

"Why don't you take Molly and drive over to Eagles Nest in June and check out those anomalies you found? If you have the right site, possibly you may find some spillage from treasure hunters who were recovering the treasure at night and possibly they missed a bar of silver or gold in their haste to clean out the hole and get out of the mountains with their treasure. Who knows maybe you might find something which will put a smile on your face, though you never know if it will bring you to tears."

Dancing Wind drove over to see Molly and there to her surprise she met Molly's new boyfriend. Senor Gonzales was a handsome Hispanic teenager, who took ones breath away. Dancing Wind walked up and gave him a hug. Molly's eyes flashed little daggers at her as she felt Dancing Wind had given senor Gonzales a lot longer hug than what was called for when first meeting new a friend. Gonzales' choice of clothing ran to the darker side. He wore a black loose fitting silk shirt, black paints and shiny black riding boots. He looked stunning in them.

Smiling and turning on the charm and the complements, Gonzales invited Dancing Wind and Molly out to lunch, and over lunch he expressed an interest in going tracking with the teenagers, so Dancing Wind invited Molly and Gonzales to go with her and explore the anomalies she had viewed thought satellite images.

Two weeks later, in mid-June, they drove out east of the town of Black Lake and driving to the southeast they found a location where they could hike over to the east canyon rim and explore the anomalies they had located on the satellite images of the canyon. While exploring each of the anomalies Molly did indeed realize that Dancing Wind was correct as the anomalies turned out to be Spanish or Jesuit markers. Off three of the five markers Molly and Dancing Wind were able to get compass directions which let them to a series of three compass stones laid out in a triangle. The following day the three explores returned to the triangle and spent the day measuring the circumference of the triangle from center to center of each compass stone. The distance of the total circumference was the distance they measured south from the primary or southernmost compass stone.

*****A compass stone is a 1,000-5,000 pound stone raised up off the ground on a stone base. Then, smaller foot-high stones hold the top stone up, leaving an air gap underneath the stone. Compass stones give either a direction to travel or exact directions to an underground treasure storage site. Note the twenty-foot-tall pine trees, for scale.*****

Dancing Wind told Molly and Gonzales that next week she had already made plans to go tracking with a old friend but the following weekend she would be free and they could return to the compass stones and once they determined the master monument they would measure on the ground to the spot they would dig to try and locate the buried treasure.

Molly did not mind the delay as it allowed her to spend more time with her new boyfriend, Gonzales. They would have plenty of time to visit the theaters and have dinners out together.

****

Two weeks passed in a flash, and the three treasure hunters returned to the three Compass stones. Measuring south for three hundred yards, Molly excitedly marked the spot to dig. Then Dancing Wind scanned the site with a metal detector and all three treasure hunters had broad smiles as the five foot square search coil screamed over the spot. It amazed Gonzales that they had measured within two feet of where the metal detector indicated there was buried metal.

Gonzales had the teenagers stand back while he used a pick and a shovel to dig a hole six feet deep and there they found six golden bars of treasure. Gonzales told the Molly and Dancing Wind he would load the gold in his back pack and haul it back to their vehicles while they filled in the hole. Then they would all meet at the vehicles.

So while both of the teenager girls removed all trace of the hole by filling it in with loose dirt, Gonzales had the more difficult job of carrying the gold to the vehicles. Then he would have to watch over his black pickup and their jeep until they arrived.

An hour later Molly and Dancing Wind arrived back at their jeep, all five tires were flat. Gonzales, his pickup truck, and the treasure they had dug up was gone!

There was nothing to do but start walking back to the town of Eagles Nest. As they walked down the dirt road an old Ford diesel truck met them and Molly and Dancing Wind smiled as Dan picked them up. Dan told them he was just dropping by to check on them and see how their tracking was coming along. Returning to the site where they had parked the jeep Dan helped his tracking students remove the five tires and load them in the back of his truck to take to town for repair. All five valve stems had been cut with a knife.

The following day Dan, Molly and Dancing Wind returned to the jeep and installed the five tires and then Dan asked Molly and Dancing Wind to show him the three compass stones set up in a triangle.

Molly replied, "It is a waste of time, all the gold is gone now!"

Dan replied, "Maybe your right, but I like to track the trails for myself just to be sure. Did you search the center of the triangle?"

Molly replied, "I never thought of that."

So, while Dan removed his metal detector for his old Ford, Molly and Dancing Wind also removed their pulse induction metal detector with its five foot search coil and walked beside Dan only five feet away. As they walked through the grassy meadow they were searching a path ten feet wide. An hour later both their search coils rang out as the metal detectors detected metal. The location was one spot centered right between their two metal detectors.

Digging a hole six feet deep took them four hours. They moved hard and fast when they realized it was not a surface indication of metal but a target down deep. There in the bottom of the hole they dug was 100 ounces of placer gold! After filling in the hole Dan, Molly and Dancing Wind walked back to their vehicles. Dan noticed his tracking students black mood he had first observed as they were walking to town the day before had been replaced by smiles.

In Eagles Nest they pulled into a small diner for dinner and Dan accompanied the two teenagers to a table for dinner, one old woman walked by him and said under her breath, "Aren't you a little old for them."

Two teenage boys walked by and one said to the other, "How does an old man like that pick up two young chicks?"

Dan just grinned at his two friends and asked, "Who's buying the steaks this time?"

****

Senor Gonzales pulled into Dallas, Texas to sell his six finger bars of gold bullion. He smiled as he thought of the new Porsche his wealth would allow him to buy. Those two teenagers were probably still working on fixing their flat tires. He could not believe how easy it had been to steal all the gold. It was like taking candy from a baby. They never suspected a thing as he loaded up all the gold bars in his back pack and said he would meet them back at the vehicles.

At the coin shop, Gonzales insisted on talking to Steve, the store manager. Steve had always been good about buying gold and silver coins with no questions asked. Gonzales emptied out his backpack and six metal bars landed on the wooden table in Steve's office.

Gonzales told Steve, "I want three hundred thousand in cash for this lot."

Steve picked up one of the golden metal bars and carefully examined it with a magnifying glass.

Steve started to suddenly laugh and, turning to Gonzales, he asked, "How was your trip to Disneyland?"

Gonzales replied, "What are you talking about?"

Steve just laughed and laughed as he examined all the gold bars. Pointing to one of the golden bars, Steve handed Gonzales his magnifying glass. There is small print on the side of each of the metal bars was stamped:

"Property of Disneyland—one pretend gold bar."

*"Ask and it shall be given you; seek and ye shall find;
knock and it shall be opened unto you."—Luke 11:9
"For everyone that asketh receiveth; and he that
seeketh findeth; and to him that knocketh it shall
be opened."—Proverbs 8:17*

Egoorcs the Scrooge

Egoorcs was a man who was reluctant to part with a dollar. His neighbors would say he still had the first dollar he had ever earned. If you went to borrow a lawn mower from Egoorcs he would insist you pay him for the gas in the lawn mower before you even started the engine. Then Egoorcs would insist you just pay $20 for the three cups of gas the tiny lawn mower engines held. If a neighbor wanted to borrow a tool Egoorcs was always ready to lend a tool such as a rake or a shove. You just had to pay a $20 dollar deposit to borrow the tool. Then when you brought the tool back he would insist you only gave him a $10 as a deposit so he pocketed $10 of his neighbors' money whenever they reluctantly borrowed a tool.

Egoorcs owned a small auto repair business which generated a steady cash flow. To increase profits in his shop he only employed illegal Mexican workers. He knew his illegal workers would never file taxes as he warned each new employee that if they filed a tax return then immigration would know how to find them and they would be deported back to Mexico. This ensured that when Egoorcs deducted the state, federal and social security taxes from all his employees paychecks that instead of his wasting all that money by giving it to the government he could just put it into his own pocket.

When Egoorcs ordered parts for the customer to repair their automobile he always inflated the cost of the parts so for each part ordered he doubled his money. If a car needed a $150 alternator, when Egoorcs wrote up the work order, that same alternator would suddenly cost $ 300.

Then Egoorcs also had to figure in the labor cost to the work order. Since he paid his illegal workers ten dollars an hour for mechanic work Egoorcs felt he was entitled to at least a modest three hundred percent profit on the labor, so he billed his mechanics at forty dollars an hour.

Egoorcs did not believing in wasting money. When his son Jimmy or his daughter Nancy need clothes for attending high school he would take them down to the Salvation Army to select what they needed. After work he would pick up Jimmy and Sarah and do the grocery shopping. Driving behind the supermarkets Egoorcs would wait in his car while he ordered Jimmy and Nancy to search the dumpsters for outdated food and dented cans the grocery store and thrown out.

On his wife's birthday Egoorcs invited his darling wife out for dinner. With misgivings she reluctantly accepted her husband's invitation for a meal out of the house where she did not have to cook the meal or wash the dishes. Egoorcs drove his wife down town to the Homeless Mission where they served free meals to the homeless street people and the poor. Egoorcs figured why waste his money at a fast food restaurant when you can get just as good food for free at the Homeless Mission.

Egoorcs had his favorite chair; no one else was allowed to move it or site in the chair. In the evening after work he would go straight to his favorite chair and sit down in his chair with the setting sun peaking over his shoulder as he read the paper while his wife fixed supper. After supper Egoorcs would return to his chair and watch TV until he went to bed. Never were his wife or kids allowed to use his chair. There were plenty of chairs in the kitchen and there was a couch in the living room they were welcome to use.

One evening as the family watched TV they saw a commercial for a Caribbean Vacation aboard. Megan turned to her husband and said why don't you take us an a cruise ship. Egoorcs turned to his wife and replied,

Megan that is one of the most foolish request you have ever made. It just shows you that women just do not have any common sense. We already have a mortgage payment here to pay and it cost me $225 per month. Now if we take a five day cruise, a cabin will cost us at least $225 per day. So a five day cruise is just like me having to pay five house mortgages. No one in their right mind would have five mortgages. Then there is the round trip air fare and they rob you again it would be ok to pay them once but they want to rob you twice, once for the ticket to your destination and then they will not take you back home unless you buy a second ticket from them to come home! If that were not bad enough the airlines then have a racket where you have to pay them to have baggage. Then those thieves will charge you by the pound if you carry three suitcases aboard the airplane. Why dealing with the airlines is like dealing with a bunch of pickpockets. People in my shop have told me they have packed expensive cameras and video recorders in their suit cases and when they arrive at their destination the electronics are gone! Then the airlines tell you they are not responsible for any stolen electronics or cameras that you entrusted them with.

Megan realized that there was no way she could talk her husband into a cruise ship vacation.

Two years later, Megan again tried to talk her husband into taking vacation, this time driving an hour to Padre Island, Texas. Maybe by driving and not taking an airplane or getting on a cruise ship, she could talk her husband into taking a lower cost vacation.

When Egoorcs finished listening to his wife's proposal of a week on the beach, he replied, "I do not know how you come up with these stupid ideas. If we drive down there, I will have all this wear and tear on my car and we will have to buy gas all the way down there and then all the way back. That is like paying for the gas twice. The oil companies at the service stations will rip us off selling us gas to go there then they will want to cheat us by making us pay for gas to go home. That is paying for the gas twice. Only a foolish woman would pay for gas twice. Certainly I won't.

"Then, when we get to Padre Island, they have you over a barrel. We will have to get a hotel room for the four of us. Did you know they will charge me for the room and then they will charge for my wife and the two kids. That is like paying for the room four times! They prey on gullible tourists charging outrageous fees just to spend the night. While for a hotel room it will cost us over a hundred dollars. If we stayed ten days they would charge us over a thousand dollars. Why that is like paying four mortgage payments. Only a fool would get into four more mortgage payments. Your idea of a vacation to Padre Island is just out of the question."

Megan ran away from her husband to the bedroom in tears.

Egoorcs walked to the bedroom door and found it locked. Yelling through the door to comfort his wife, he added, "Honey, I am just doing you a favor. There is no point in driving to the beach in the summer as probably a hurricane will come and we will be lucky to escape with our lives. You know there is no point going to the beach in winter as it is too cold to swim."

Egoorcs was always on the lookout for a way to make a dollar. One day over lunch, Egoorcs overheard his employees talking about Spanish Treasure, search for the treasure which failed as well as successful treasure hunts. Stories of treasure Galleons loaded with gold and silver filled his mind and soon Egoorcs had caught an incurable disease, commonly called gold fever. Carefully talking with his workers he learned that they believed that there was a Spanish treasure buried near the San Sabe Mission. Even Frank Dobie had published some authentic ancient treasure maps in his books.

The story often told was that there were three silver treasures buried just before the Spanish Mission was attacked by Indians. So during the spring and summer after closing his automotive shop for the day Egoorcs would drive to San Sabe looking for his silver treasures. Four months of driving the roads near San Sabe, four flat tires and replacing all his bald tires resulted in Egoorcs realizing he was no closer to finding his treasure, now that four months earlier. Egoorcs decided that finding treasure was simply too much work.

Two of Egoorcs' auto mechanics from Mexico decided to file an American tax return to get back some of the money that Egoorcs had withheld from their pay. Unfortunately they were dismayed to learn that all they money that had been withheld had been pocketed by their boss so none went to the state or federal government.

When they confronted Egoorcs about the thousands of dollars he had kept from their paychecks, Egoorcs told his employees, "You're lucky you have a job. If any of you complain about what I withhold from your pay, I will just call immigration and have you thrown into jail as you're in this country illegally and none of you have a green card."

Several months later, Pancho and Juan learned of Egoorcs' treasure-hunting trips so, over lunch, they told Egoorcs the story of the wonderful treasure they had discovered in the Sierra Madre Mountains of Mexico, before they came to the United States.

Several years ago they had been in the Sierra Madre Mountains hunting Havalinas (wild pigs) to cook for a fiesta, when suddenly a storm came up. Looking for any possible shelter on the mountain they had been hunting upon they found a cave going back about thirty feet. In the back of this cave was a wooden chest about three feet wide, four feet long and three feet high made of stout wood and strengthened by heavy black iron bands every 6 inches. Pulling with all their might to take the treasure chest out of the cave was impossible; they could not move the treasure chest even one inch.

So the two friends resolved to go to town and borrow a mule to haul the treasure chest to town. Bringing a mule back to their cave with the treasure chest was their second attempt to recover the treasure. Using the mules harness and some sturdy rope they attached the mule to the treasure chest. Next they went to lead the mule out of the cave but the mule simply could not pull the treasure chest. Getting mad at the mule the men whipped the mule and it surged forward six inches. Whipping it again and again only got them a few more inches. At this rate the men realized the treasure chest was simply too heavy for the mule to pull.

We discussed the situation and we resolved that the only way we were going to be able to recover this treasure was take sludge hammers and break open the treasure chest, then take the contents and load it on the back of a jeep. So here we are, we came to America to work and save money to buy a jeep. Then we can return to the Sierra Madre Mountains and recover the treasure chest. Yet such is life; we have worked here for you three years senor Egoorcs and try as we might we have not been able to afford a jeep so we can recover our treasure. If you would give us a jeep and the money for gas and food we would go down to the mountains and recover the treasure and in exchange for your help we would give you half of the treasure. It need not be a new jeep wrangler but it has to be a dependable jeep to take us through the rugged mountains and be able to carry the treasure right back here. Then you could help us sell the treasure.

For several weeks Egoorcs kept thinking of the story and soon in his thoughts all he could think of was a treasure chest overflowing with thousands of gold coins. What luck, that two of his employees told him about the treasure they found. Egoorcs began looking for a used four wheel drive jeep so as to enable his two employees to recover his treasure. Finding a jeep in good condition he purchased it for three thousand five hundred dollars. Then he told Poncho and Juan he would expect them back in two weeks with his treasure. Pancho and Juan insisted on at least gas for the trip. They told their boss they would pay for all their meals out of their own pocket but it was only fair since they were giving him half the treasure that he should pay for the gas.

Getting the four hundred dollars for gas was a difficult decision for Egoorcs but he reasoned when his employees return with my treasure, he would become a very rich man. Why maybe he would even give Poncho and Juan a tiny portion of his treasure.

Poncho and Juan were extremely happy with the jeep and the four hundred dollars they had for expenses. Loading up all their belongings they were off to see their families in Durango, located on the lower end of the Sierra Madre Occidental. Durango is one jumping off point for prospectors exploring the Sierra Madre Mountains.

When they arrived in Durango, Poncho and Juan went straight to their casas (houses) to see their families. It had been so long since they had been able to return and kiss their wives and hug their children. Over dinner the two families celebrated their husbands return. Over dinner, Pancho talked about how the United States was a land of opportunity. Sometimes though there were crooks in Los Ustados Unitidos, just like in Mexico, who tried to cheat you out of your money. The ruse their grandfather used to get his first pickup truck still worked. By telling their boss about a cave full of treasure they had been able to get their boss to give them this nice jeep they now drove.

****20 years later****

Dancing Wind and Molly O'Brian were driving down the highway 37 between San Antonio and Corpus Christi, Texas when off to the right side of the road Dancing Wind saw an Angel sticking out her thumb hitch hiking. For a moment Dancing Wind was speechless as her jeep passed the hitchhiker with the pair of wings. Then she flipped on her blinker, hit the brakes and pulled off to the side of the road.

Molly said, "Don't tell me you saw her, too."

Then both teenagers got out of their jeep and walked back to the Angel by the side of the road. The Angle was beautiful but they were not sure if the Angel was male or female for she seemed to not clearly be either sex. When the Angle spoke, it was not what one heard for there were no words spoken aloud, instead the Angles words were heard inside their heads.

Simply the Angel said, "I was looking for a ride."

Now both Dancing Wind and Molly knew there was a lot more to it than the simple request the Angel made, for an Angel has the ability to travel where ever they wish at the speed of thought. For it is true that an Angel can be or go anywhere instantly. So for some reason the Angel had chosen to ride with them.

Both teenagers speaking at once instantly replied, "You're welcome to travel with us. We will take you wherever you want to go."

As the jeep traveled down highway 37 towards Corpus Christi as they approached an upcoming exit the Angel said, "This is my exit."

Without thinking, Dancing Wind put on her blinker and took the exit. Off to the right she saw a service station and a restaurant. Dancing Wind had no intention of leaving the Angel standing alongside of the road. She would take the Angel where ever the Angel chose to go.

The Angel then said, by putting the thoughts in their mind, "Why don't you fill up the gas tank?"

Then, as they pulled up to the pumps, Molly turned to ask the Angel a question and she simply disappeared as if she had never ridden in their vehicle.

Dancing Wind saw the Angel simply disappear, then turning to Molly she said, "Well I guess we will take our guests advice and fill up our gas tank."

Molly went in to pay for the gas while Dancing Wind pumped the gas and cleaned the hundreds of moths off her windshield. While pumping gas she heard the sound, it was the sound of a starter cranking and cranking while the car refused to start. The battery got weaker and weaker and soon would turn the engine over no more. The car battery was dead.

Out of the car came a middle age woman, she was crying. She was a woman whom seemed lost and without hope. The station manager told her she would have to move her car away from the pumps, but he kindly added she could leave it overnight in one of the parking spaces off to the side. Dancing Wind, Molly and two men helped push the woman's car as she steered it away from the gas pumps into a parking space.

As the woman sat in her car she sobbed and repeatedly cried out, "Oh GOD what am I to do? I just can't make it any more."

Molly asked her "Can I give you a ride home or take you anywhere?"

Looking up at Molly and wiping the tears away from her face Megan asked for a ride home. So Molly and Dancing Wind drove Megan home. During the drive home they learned she was a widow whose husband Egoorcs had died five years earlier.

Arriving at a single wide trailer, badly in need of repairs, Megan invited Dancing Wind and Molly into her house for coffee or tea. Accepting her offer they walked into the living room as they waited for the water on the stove to boil. Molly told them to have a seat while she fixed the coffee and so Molly sat down on the couch and almost hit the floor. All the springs were busted and the couch frame seemed broken. Dancing Wind sat in a broken down chair facing the TV. The springs were broken, the cushion was lumpy and Dancing Wind wiggled her body trying to get comfortable.

Then Megan arrived bringing them each a cup of coffee. Over coffee she told them her husband had died five years earlier leaving her nothing accept this old trailer and two acres of land. The fifteen year old car with 290,000 miles had just died at the service station. She got by waitressing at the diner on tips and now she felt she was at the end of the line. Her emergency savings consisted of a twenty dollar bill.

Dancing Wind did not know what to do or say. She knew the woman was in desperate straits, and really needed a new car and a decent paying job.

Silently Dancing Wind began praying for guidance, for Dancing Wind simply did not know how to help the woman.

Suddenly Dancing Winds Guardian Angel, Lily appeared and said to Dancing Wind, "Tear the chair cushion."

Out loud, Dancing Wind asked Lily, "Tear the chair cushion?" That did not make any sense at all.

Molly looked at Dancing Wind, a question in her eyes.

Megan looked at Dancing Wind, thinking that was a crazy thing to say out of the blue.

Out loud again Dancing Wind questioned Lily, "Tear the chair cushion?"

Again the Guardian Angel told Dancing Wind, "Tear the chair cushion"

Dancing Wind got up from the lumpy chair cushion and grabbing the material in her fist she pulled ripping the fabric.

Bundles of money scattered everywhere, the bundles of money consisted of rolls of tens, twenties, fifties.

Dancing Wind was frozen as the money fell all about her.

Then Dancing Wind heard Lily say, "Tear the chair apart. Tear the chair apart now!"

Then Dancing Wind tore the fabric from the arm rest, more piles of money scattered all about the floor.

Megan stood up from the couch and walked over to Dancing Wind and looking at the money scattered everywhere all she could say was, "Oh my GOD. Oh, my GOD!" over and over.

Dancing Wind, following the Angels counsel, had discovered Megan's deceased husband's bank, he kept all his money hidden in the chair he sat in as he watched TV every night.

An Angel may see a site (such as a spring in the mountains or a desert oasis) with three different views: as it was in the past, as it is now, and as it may be in the future.

The view of the future is not always set in stone. It can be shaped by the actions of mankind. When men and women work in harmony with nature spirits it sends out a positive vibration across the land.

The Coconut Trees of the California Desert

Robert squinted in the bright sunlight. Sweat ran down his forehead and stung his eyes. The sun seemed to bake the earth. He could feel both the heat beating down upon him as well as the heat rising up off the ground he walked upon. Robert imagined dying of thirst out in this desert.

The weather forecast predicted a sweltering 116 degrees. "Drink plenty of water and stay in the shade!" was advised.

"There is no shade in this god forsaken desert!" thought Robert. The truth of the matter was that he needed water. Without it he would not last the day.

Robert had not thought about the consequences of running out of water ever before, but he had plenty of time to consider it as he followed his partner John through the desert. The two men walked without talking. Robert did not have the energy to look at the terrain and plan a route of travel. He imagined turning right around and heading back to his truck. I may have a better chance of getting out of here alive if I turned back instead of following this fool, he thought. Robert was sure he could find the group of vehicles where he had parked. He remembered the extra water and sunscreen that the others had left behind in their vehicles. Those idiots had taken so much time to slather themselves with protective sunscreen and fill their stupid canteens.

John carried a half gallon of water for the walk along the west side of the mesa looking for Spanish trail markers. Gradually over the last four hours John had drunk the entire contents of his canteen. Beside him walked Robert whom seemed definitely thirsty, and suffering in the heat. John knew that one cannot walk through the desert without water. John had overheard Dancing Wind talking to Robert about carrying water.

John had the urge to tell Robert what he thought of his intelligence, or more correctly, his complete lack thereof. Then upon reflection he thought he would simply let the desert teach Robert about water. The desert can be a mighty hard teacher when it comes to water. John had offered Robert some sunscreen when they were back at the vehicles. Robert refused with a curse and added that he would not put that white cream on his clean skin as he did not want to get messy.

"Besides," Robert said, "I never get sun burned." It looked to John, like Robert face and arms were getting badly sunburned now.

Even though Robert had not brought a canteen on the trip, he found himself carrying an empty canteen. It belonged to their instructor Dancing Wind. She had offered to let him use one or two of hers, but he had refused saying, "I can go all day without water."

Dancing Wind asked Robert, "Would you to carry an extra canteen of water for me?" The canteen was hanging on his shoulder, without a single drop inside. Dancing Wind was a beautiful woman, but she must have been crazy for bringing him into this desert.

Robert really wanted to turn around and follow the east mesa to his car. He figured it would take about five hours; should he last that long in the desert heat. Robert was not sure he could walk the way he had just come without any water at all. The sun was almost south of them now and was barely casting any shadows so it had to be about eleven. The next couple of hours would be the hottest part of the day. Robert thought about his reason for taking this trip into the desert.

Locating a treasure sounded so easy when he read the stories about tracking. You just follow the Spanish Trail to the treasure site, and then pick up the treasure. It sounded so easy even a fool to do it. When he reached the north end of the mesa, all he had for

Dancing Wind was an empty canteen instead of the full canteen that he told her he would carry for her. Well she would never let him go prospecting with her again! He wasn't sure it mattered anyway, since he might not make it back alive. Robert decided if he lived, he was going to see an attorney. He was going to sue Dancing Wind for asking him to carry her canteen so he was unable to carry one of his own, and he would sue the sun too for giving him this sunburn. Already his arms, face and nose were sunburned.

It was all he could do to put one foot in front of another and keep on moving. Robert was tired. The rocks he tried to sit down upon to rest started to burn him right through his paints and he jumped up off them. He was so tired and hot. Never did Robert imagine that tracking a Spanish trail through the Mojave Desert would ever be like this. Never had he ever been so hot, tired and thirsty.

John the other beginning tracking student laughed when he jumped off the hot black rock he had just sat down upon for a moment to rest. Robert's throat was so dry he did not have the energy or moisture to laugh or even talk.

Meanwhile, Dancing Wind was tracking with Jean and Mary across the canyon. The women took lots of pictures. They had discovered lots of different markers and had even found an ancient stone map to a nearby source of water! Dancing Wind did not think that the group should separate, but Robert had insisted. He thought they could cover more ground if they split into two groups. Dancing Wind was not happy about the arrangement, but she knew that each student had a lesson they chose to learn on this outing.

Suddenly, Robert noticed John had abruptly changed direction. Looking around for a reason, Robert noticed that John had spotted the three women about 300 yards away, slightly north of the mesa. Robert and John picked up their pace as they headed straight for the three women. At 100 yards away Robert started waving his arms. He tried to yell "water, water," but his voice came out as a quiet whisper.

Robert had told Dancing Wind that he could walk all day without water. In fact he said, "I've never purchased a canteen because I've never felt the need to carry one. Why should I waste the money to buy a canteen if I don't need one."

She had just smiled at him and replied, "It's your choice." She had asked him to carry a canteen for her, as she told him that she really guzzled water when out in the desert and he had reluctantly agreed to help her.

Robert had drunk the canteen of water he had told Dancing Wind that he would carry for her. He had emptied it down to the last drop of water.

He had not meant to drink all her water but the heat was just so intense. After thirty minutes of walking in this heat, he just had to have a little water. He opened Dancing Wind's canteen he carried and just took a few sips. She would not miss the water and obviously he needed it worse right now. Forty-five minutes later all he could think about was the water he heard sloshing back and forth in the canteen as he walked. The sun baked him like he was in a hot blast furnace. He could not go any longer without the water so he again drank the water he carried for Dancing Wind. Four hours later, the half gallon of water was just a bad memory of his word and how he had broken his promise.

It was just a simple tracking exercise. Four tracking students of assorted ages were traveling with Dancing Wind as they followed a segment of the Old Spanish Trail. The two groups agreed to meet up on the north end of the mesa in four or five hours and compare notes about what they had found.

As they approached Dancing Wind, Robert croaked "Water, water!"

Dancing Wind smiled and told Robert, "I never intended for you to carry the canteen all morning and never take a sip of water. You are welcome to the water in the canteen you are carrying for me."

Robert replied, "That canteen has been empty for hours, how much water is left in your canteen?"

Dancing Wind replied, "I have a few sips of water left in the canteen that I have been carrying. I will take a drink and let you have the rest." Dancing Wind would not have handed Robert her canteen without taking a few sips first, in case Robert drank all her water too and left her with nothing.

Dancing Wind asked the students to describe the Spanish trail markers they had seen. Robert and John reported that they had seen no Spanish Markers on the west side of the mesa. Jean and Mary drew in the sand a sketch of the three Spanish markers they had seen. One was a four foot high cairn of lava rocks, beside the cairn was a smaller rock with a church cross and the letters: "ORO," which Dancing Wind told the group meant gold or silver. The cross meant it was property of the church. The third Spanish marker was a stone map showing some Spanish mines, a heart, a steep slope and an area with water.

Based on the map which had been chiseled into the rocks, they needed to travel to the northwest. Within an hour they would arrive at the water source depicted on the map. Robert listened to their plan. He thought it was ridiculous to follow the directions off a set of ancient pictographs to find water. He knew they were in trouble. Already they had gone too far in the desert for the limited water they carried was already gone. To walk further out into the desert was committing suicide. He knew they would never get out of the desert alive.

As Robert watched, Dancing Wind walked further into the Mojave Desert following the directions she had read on the ancient stone pictograph.

Jean, Mary and John followed along behind her. Robert watched Dancing Wind leading the way further into the desert. She's crazy he thought. Their canteens were empty! Robert looked at the way back to where his car was parked. No, he guessed he would not reach his car alive, not with an empty canteen in this heat. Reluctantly Robert followed along behind the group as they moved further out into the Mojave Desert. An hour slowly passed and then Dancing Wind pointed to a stone turtle beside the trail.

She explained to the students, "The turtle is an ancient symbol often used to indicate the direction to water. Later on the Spanish used the turtle symbol to indicate the direction to gold or silver. When following Spanish symbols special care must be to observe the head, tail and legs as often one of these was used to indicate the direction to travel to a Spanish mine, treasure, water or campsite."

Mary noticed a change in vegetation. The cactus was giving way to scattered patches of grass and yucca. Thirty minutes later she saw the tops of the trees. As she pointed this out to everyone, they shifted their line of travel slightly to head directly for the green trees growing around the desert oasis.

At the base of a small mountain was a small oasis surround by approximately two dozen trees. There were coconut trees, palm trees, and a few lemon trees. Never had Dancing Wind's students expected to find the fruit trees around the desert oasis. Dancing Wind filled up her canteen from the small trickle of water flowing out of the earth.

Then she walked over to the lemon tree which was about her height. Carefully she reached in towards a branch, avoiding the long sharp thorns and firmly grabbed a yellow lemon. Twisting the lemon, it easily came off the lemon tree. Dancing Wind then took her pocket knife and sliced the lemon in half. Half the lemon she squeezed into her canteen of water. Then she removed the seeds and planted them almost a foot deep around the oasis. Mary grabbed the second half of Dancing Winds lemon and squeezed the tangy juice into her canteen then she, too, copied Dancing Wind and planted the seeds from the lemon. Soon everyone was picking the lemons and squeezing the juice into their canteens.

Dancing Wind told everyone to rest in the shade and to drink all the water they craved. She told everyone that they would rest for two hours then walk out after the hottest time of the day had passed. Dancing Wind found a comfortable spot in the shade and rested her head on an oval or rounded shape of black plastic mostly buried in the dirt. While she rested with her eyes closed she listened to the discussion which was occurring between Robert, John, Jean and Mary.

Robert was explaining that long ago this land was under the sea. The Polynesians' came here and at the edge of the hills must have been the shore line. Here they planted the coconut trees so that should they return again there would always be food for them. Over the centuries as the land dried up and the sea water disappeared, the land turned into a desert and these few coconut trees are the last remnants of the Polynesians traveling here.

Jean thought maybe the palm trees came here from Israel. The lost tribe of Israel settled here in California because of the similar weather to Israel and they brought the palm trees here from their homeland. "That is why there are Palm trees in California," Jean said. "The Lost Tribe of Israel brought them."

John thought the lemons came from Florida, the Caribbean or Central America. Possibly centuries ago this desert was connected to the Sea of Cortez, and storms washed lemon trees up here along the ancient shoreline where they have been growing for centuries. As the ancient sea dried up it left a legacy of lemon trees growing out here in the desert.

After taking a nap to allow the sun to begin setting, and to allow the desert to begin to cool down a little, Dancing Wind told everyone to take a last drink of water and fill up their canteens.

"We will be walking back to our parked vehicles," she told everyone. "Before we leave I would like you to help me pick up any trash that is lying around. We should always try to leave a place better than we found it."

As the tracking students picked up the trash, Mary smiled and winked as she saw Dancing Wind filling her pack with a dozen large plastic nursery pots which she was packing out from the oasis. Dancing Wind caught her smile and she smiled back. So Mary walked over to where Dancing Wind had picked up the plastic pots half buried in the sand she bent down to the ground and picked up the plastic nursery tags from two California tree nurseries and she slipped the name tags of the trees into her backpack with the trash she had collected.

Mother Earth needs our help to clean up our environment and help her restore our environment. It is the little acts like picking up trash and planting trees, which will in the end, determine if we as a people will continue to live here, or if we will continue down a path of destruction of our Ecosystem. The actions you choose, or fail to choose to put into practice may, in the end, determine whether our children inherit a paradise her on earth or a barren wasteland. So tell me, or more importantly tell the Angel sitting beside you, what you have resolved to do to help Mother Earth this month. Then go out and put a smile on your Guardian Angel's face. For it is in acts of love, acts of charity and acts to help the environment that you are also strengthen the bond or your connection to your own Guardian Angel.

As the students retraced their route back to their parked vehicles they reflected upon the day's events. The last rays of the sunlight were fading and it would be dark soon. Like a few other students in the past, Robert could not get out of this hell hole called the Mojave Desert fast enough. Robert would always feel most comfortable in the city where he grew up.

For some like Jean and John, they would follow these trails a time or two. They would become memories they would tell a friend or their children. For a woman like Mary, her experience was like the awakening of her spirit. Mary felt like she was finally coming alive. And Dancing Wind tells me that it is in

the awakening of the spirit where personal growth,
love, and even the keys to heaven itself may be found!

The Angel wondered if his charge had the honor and integrity
To give 25% of a recovery to charity, as the individual had promised.
So, before taking his charge up onto the mountains
to look for a buried treasure, the Angel arranged a test.
The Angel had his charge go to a bank and cash a check;
If his charge kept the extra money the bank teller over-paid him,
The trip into the mountains would only result in enjoying the scenery.
If his charge returned the excess money the bank teller accidently over-paid him,
Then the Angel knew the individual he watched over would honor his word.
And thus the result of the test of honor was used to determine the path
The Angel would lead the person he watched over as they traveled through the mountains.

The Priest

Juan was a Franciscan priest who was a child at heart. He loved to play games with children. Since his lay brothers felt that Juan lacked the maturity and dignity the order required he was sent from Mexico City north to the northern frontier outpost of Taos.

At the Taos mission Juan was assigned chores to his superiors felt he was most suited. Instead of leading the adult congregation in prayer Juan would be assigned to watch over the children while their parents were attending church.

During the week Juan would be found attending the gardening, pulling weeds, caring for the fruit trees and when time allowed he loved to play with the children. As the years passed it became clear to all the Franciscans that Juan had no desire to lead the congregation in prayer, he rather would be found playing with the children or working in the garden.

And then came the dreaded news from Mexico City of the outbreak of small pox. Small pox is a disease leaving blisters over the entire body. All these blisters itched horribly, and when scratched, rapidly spread the disease over the entire body of the individual. Frequently, the individuals died from this disease and anything they touched or handled became infected and spread the disease to new people. Especially among the Native Americans there was no resistance to this disease so the mortality rate approached 90%.

When the news of the outbreak of small pox in Mexico City occurred, many people fled to the four winds fleeing this disease. Some of these individuals had already contracted the disease and did not realize it yet, so they served as disease carriers rapidly spreading the small pox. Some individuals were sold the clothing or blankets of the men and woman who died from the disease by unscrupulous men. Anyone who unknowingly purchased the clothing from infected victims quickly caught the disease too.

It was only a matter of time when the small pox spread to the frontiers of the Spanish Empire and came to Taos. The disease spread like wild fire among the Native Americans. When any individual caught the disease it quickly spread to all who cared for the sick or came into contact with them.

To try and stop the spread of the disease desperate measures were taken, all who showed any symptoms were quarantined well away from the Taos Pueblo where they lived.

These sick individuals were sent over to the Taos gorge to stay so they would not infect the healthy members of the tribe. Husbands were separated from their wives, children were taken from their families and ordered to stay away until they recovered from the disease or died. At first the quarantined people were taken food but as the disease spread death everywhere soon the sick individuals were no longer taken food as some tribal members were afraid to take food as they were scared of the disease and the few remaining tribal members who would bring food to the sick and dying were not able to meet the food demands required to feed hundreds of sick tribal members.

Juan took it upon himself to care for hundreds of these orphan children. The children he had laughed and played with, he washed, and bathed them down on the Rio Grande. He fixed them soup and spoon fed them, he prayed to GOD for them and despite his best care, they died in his arms and he buried them. Child after child he tried to help. It was no use, he knew of no cure for small pox, and each time a child died in his arms he cried out his heart.

Soon Juan too contracted the awful disease, within two weeks he was blind. In four weeks he was dead there beside dozens of Indian children he had done his best to care for.

Juan spirit remained along the gorge where he and the children he cared for died. His love of life disappeared, his love of children turned to tears, his love and his memory of those days of tears engulfed Juan's spirit. Sometimes the west winds carried story of his grief and sadness.

To everything there is a time and a place and a season. When the Wind Spirits carried the story of Juan the priest to a Lakota Medicine man he realized that Juan was unable to let go of his grief as he was engulfed in his despair. So Dan told Dancing Wind they needed to return to the Taos Gorge to complete some unfinished spirit work.

To the north they traveled in the fall of the year. When the nights begin to freeze and the aspen has turned yellow and the Canadian geese are flying south they came to the Rio Grande Gorge several miles south of the Dunn Bridge to a location above the old stage coach hot springs. Here on the east side of the gorge in the BLM Wild River recreational area they traveled to a place above the hot springs where the gray dirt lies and the land has begun to drop due to faulting they looked for their old medicine circles to perform their spirit work.

The old medicine circles used on previous occasions had been destroyed. Their locations only remained in the heart and the memory of a Lakota medicine man and the teenager he was teaching the path of the spirit to. Dancing Wind and Dan gathered up fist size stones to make a new medicine wheel. There on the edge of the high gray and black cliffs they made a circle of stones about ten feet around.

Into this circle they made a opening in the stones, a door way if you wish to call it that which faced to the east. Around the inside edges, close to the rocks forming the medicine circle they placed small twelve inch high burning sticks of incense. In the center of the medicine circle a small fire was lit using rosen, sage and frankincense. Dancing Wind and Dan sat on the west side of the medicine wheel with their backs against the stones. They both faced east towards the open door of the medicine wheel. At the time of day when the sun broke the Sangre De Cristo Mountain tops to the east the medicine man nodded to Dancing Wind to begin drumming slowly. She watched his fingers to ensure she had the proper slow rhythm. For his index finger was indicating the proper slow rhythm for her to beat the drum.

Slowly at first one Native American child's spirit entered the medicine circle as Dan and Dancing Wind said their sacred prayers from their heart to the Great Spirit. As one child after another entered the circle and began walking around the prayer circle in a clockwise manner, a child led the blind priest Juan into the circle with them.

Dancing Wind had continued drumming slowly as Dan prayed to the Great Spirit to open his arms and accept his children back *home.* When the Angels indicated everyone had arrived who chose to return *home* then Dan indicated with his index finger for Dancing Wind to slowly increase the drum beat. Dan continued his prayers and Dancing Wind prayed too for the Angels to come and take these children *home.* As the Spirits danced around the medicine wheel suddenly a door of light appeared on the north side of the medicine wheel, into this light flew the children who had been dancing around the medicine wheel, for literally they danced right into the light of the tunnel. Holding the blind priest hand was a little Indian girls spirit whom he and cared for until her death. The little girl was leading the old priest home with her.

When the door of light closed Dan and Dancing Wind stopped their drumming and prayers. Dancing Wind and Dan got up and carefully walking clockwise they walked out of the medicine wheel. By the entrance they picked up some of their entrance rocks and used them to close the opening in the Medicine Wheel. Tears filled both of their eyes and rolled down their faces. They rolled down Dancing Winds face as she was so happy she was able to help the children and the priest return *home.*

Tears flowed down the old Lakota medicine man's weathered face as he was proud that Dancing Wind had learned her lessons so well and would be carrying on the tradition of working with the Great Spirit and helping spirits return home. He realized the next time that Dancing Wind would be performing this ceremony would be for him when he returned *home.*

There are times when life has its ups and its downs
Yet without the rocky road, one would not learn and
grow
For you have personally selected the challenges and
obstacles you chose to overcome.
They are YOUR life plan. Literally the lessons you have
chosen to learn!
Most lessons revolve around the events you are
experiencing in your life:
Love, Dignity, Honor, Integrity, Forgiveness, Sharing,
Money, Teamwork, Religion,
Prejudice, Tolerance, Peace, Perseverance, Food, Weight
issues and Friendship.
You will keep repeating these life lessons, time after
time, life after life until you incorporate
The highest course into your thoughts, actions and
deeds.

San Sebastian

San Sebastian lived in Seville, Spain and, like a few very lucky men, he had a government job. Sebastian worked long hours at the "Archivo General de Indias" (Spanish Archives), filing documents and records for the Spanish crown. Most papers contained trivial matters of little interest to San Sebastian. They contained wills of deceased, records of court proceedings, records of trials, requisitions of supplies, bills of lading, deeds or land titles. On rare occasions San Sebastian read the manifest of the precious treasures brought back to Spain aboard the treasure ships. Literally tons of treasures in the form of bars of gold, silver, jewelry, emeralds, turquoise, and jade arrived in the port cities.

For ten years San Sebastian had worked in the "Archivo General de Indias" (Spanish Archives) before and older librarian, Don Carlos noticed his avid interest in the Ships manifest of the Spanish Plate Fleet. For five years they occasionally discussed the ships manifest which detailed the entire cargo officially carried aboard the treasure ships. Don Carlos explained to San Sebastian that often up to fifty percent of the gold and silver cargo was not listed on the ships manifest, literally it was being smuggled into Spain to avoid paying the king his "Royal Fifth" (quinto) or twenty percent tax on the gold and silver.

If one were caught smuggling, the entire treasure was seized, and there were occasions where this did if fact happen. Yet often there were government officials who were willing to look the other way, when a generous contribution was made to their retirement. While bribes in gold were always well liked, silver certainly was not refused. When a tax inspector could extract a bribe equal to a year's pay that he made working for his government pay for letting a small amount of cargo slip by untaxed; most inspectors eagerly enjoyed the extra take home pay. One way of avoiding taxes was to under weigh each bar of gold or silver. The owner of the silver bars would tell the tax inspector that the silver bars with a cut mark across the top of the bar of silver are to be recorded as one hundred ounces of bullion. So a hundred and twenty ounce silver bar would be recorded as being one hundred ounces. To a casual inspector, walking by observing the process, one sees the tax inspector inventorying each bar and properly recording it and checking it on the ships manifest. If there should be two hundred of the one-hundred-ounce bars of silver, then the tax on shipment of silver bars should be four thousand ounces of silver. By under-recording the weight twenty ounces on each bar, then four thousand ounce of silver were not taxed. Four thousand ounces of silver then was smuggled into Spain tax free. Yet to the casual observer every bar of silver was properly weighted and all the taxes paid.

A hundred ounce bribe of silver often made a small shipment with some irregularities pass thought the tax or customs inspectors without difficulty. This did not happen just once in a while but was a common practice in Spanish ports. It was not just small mine owners whom paid off the inspectors but it was the normal practice for even the wealthy to arrange to bribe the tax collectors. Some estimates place the amount of smuggled cargo at fifty percent of what was officially listed on the ships manifest.

Among the items stored in the Spanish Archives were coded Spanish maps showing the exact directions to every Spanish gold, silver and emerald mine in North America, Central and South America. The maps showed the exact location of the mine, the trails to reach the mine and often where the treasure room was located. Five years passed before Don Carlos shared the secrets of reading the secret coded language with San Sebastian.

Suddenly a whole new world opened to San Sebastian as hundreds of maps suddenly came alive with to meaning and the detailed directions to the treasures laid out on the maps. Hidden mines, treasure caches, royal storehouses of treasure were all suddenly revealed by the maps when he knew how to read the codes designed to conceal the true maps contents from enemies of Spain.

One night over dinner, Don Carlos introduced San Sebastian to a group of his five most trusted and closest friends. They told San Sebastian that they had been looking for a man whom they could trust whom could turn a disaster into an opportunity that would benefit all of the group. The Indian rebellion of 1680 had thrown the entire territory of New Spain into turmoil. The Governors Palace in Santa Fe had fallen to hostile Indians. The towns of San Cristobal, Questa, Rio Honda, Taos, Espanola, San Juan, Santa Fe, Albuquerque, down to Socorro, even as far south as Las Cruces had fallen to the rebellious Indian raiders. This disaster had resulted in hundreds of mines shutting down and the deaths of hundreds of settlers and miners.

Yet to the men sitting around an old wooden dinner table in Seville this disaster, if carefully handled, could give them the opportunity to live out their lives in comfort that gold could provide them. Their plan was to carefully remove all documents relating to one of the rich mines in New Spain. Since the only other copy of the documents, were hopefully lost at the Palace of the Governors in New Spain during the Indian rebellion, what they hoped to achieve is to go back into one of the old gold mines and remove the gold bars left at the mine site when the hostile Indians rebelled and overthrew the Spanish authorities.

The archivists had carefully gone through the records to select a small mine in a relatively remote location that would have had few visits from Spanish Authorities collecting taxes, yet they wanted a rich mine that had a greater likely hood of possibly having already mined gold bars on hand at the time of the rebellion. A large mining operation was out of the question as there were simply numerous men who would have knowledge of the mines operation, as well as the trail to the mine, would allow the Spanish Authorities to easily relocate the mine and resume operation. Large mines would also have detailed records and numerous entries concerning operations and tax records from the paying of the Royal Fifth (20%) taxes to the King.

Essentially the archivists wanted to locate a small, relatively remote mine that their documents showed was a rich mine that had just started operations. Then they proposed to make the mine disappear from all official records and send one person to New Spain to recover any gold bullion and recover any rich high grade gold ore. And it was San Sebastian whom they proposed to send to New Spain to recover this gold and smuggle it back to Spain where they would each receive an equal share.

The mine which the group selected that most nearly fit this criteria was a remote mine just a day's ride north of Taos, high up on the north slope of Taos Mountain. This mine was situated above the rebellious Pueblo of Taos, whose very ringleader (Pope) instigated the rebellion against the lawful Spanish authorities. The records showed the mine had just paid the King a Royal Fifth in taxes on a shipment of gold amounting to 800 pounds of gold. That indicated the mine had just produced 4,000 pounds of gold in the last two months prior to the rebellion! There was a note in the archives that the mine was so rich that the gold vein was the thickness of large kernels of corn and a miner could remove gold with a knife. The records in the Spanish Archives indicated the mine was worked by four Spaniards and they had about fifty Indian slaves. They had been following a vein of gold a quarter of an inch thick. Records in Santa Fe, and Seville indicated that the mine owners died in the rebellion. Apparently a contingent of his majesties soldiers was sent to slaughter the rebellious Indians and make an example of them to any natives whom defied Spanish justice. Even better was the fact that they could find no records remained to explain what happened to the soldiers. Since there were no reports filed in the archives upon the return to the detachment of him Majesties soldiers to Santa Fe, possibly none of the soldiers survived the rebellion. Hopefully no one was left alive from the rebellion whom knew of the mine's existence. Yes, this mine fit the group's criteria perfectly.

****

Three months later, San Sebastian was bound for the New World. Veracruz, Mexico would be the jumping off port to begin a year long trek north into the northern frontier of New Spain. Taos was one of the northern outposts of the Spanish Empire and was known for the Taos Fair in the fall. In Taos one could encounter Pueblo Indians, Navaho's trading the wool from sheep, apaches trading slaves and furs, Ute Indians with slaves and furs trading for gun powder, horses and Taos White Lightning (whiskey). Smugglers, fur trappers, Indians slave traders, gold miners to the fur trapping could all be found at Taos. It was here in Taos that San Sebastian would build an adobe home, plant his crops, and very discretely begin looking for the rich gold mine high up on Taos Mountain's north slope close to the timber line. San Sebastian arrived in Taos late in the fall with just sufficient time to build and adobe home before winter set in. All winter long there was nothing to do but wait for the spring when the deep snow would melt. With the arrival of spring, Sebastian had to plow the fields, then irrigated the fields with water from the acequia (irrigation water flowing through a community ditch). Sebastian planted apple and apricot seed even though he was sure he would return to Spain long before the trees bore fruit.

When summer came and the snow had melted off the north face of Taos Mountain; San Sebastian made his first trip up into the mountains in June a second trip in July and a third trip in August. Then fall harvest time came and corn, pumpkins and squash had to be put away for a winter food supply. A hunting trip for Elk was planned to provide carne seca (dried meat) through the winter. Firewood needed to be cut to provide heat for the winter. With the first snows of fall the mountains became impassable until next year.

It was in the fall season when the biggest event occurred in San Sebastian's life that was truly to change in unimaginable ways; through Sebastian was not to know it at the time. Sebastian's wife Maria had a baby girl whom the proud parents named Mary after the mother of Jesus. Mary was to change Sebastian in ways he never thought possible. Yet children often have that effect upon both parents.

Every summer and fall Sebastian rode up into the mountains following the Spanish treasure monuments up into the mountains north of Taos. At first in the lower elevations the trail to the Spanish mines was clearly marked with monuments every hundred yards. Yet since the trail to the gold mine had not been used in twenty years, many changes on the trail had occurred due to the passage of time. The trail wound up higher and higher around the eastern slopes of Taos Mountain headed towards the sacred Blue Lakes. But trees had grown up over the years concealing both the Spanish Trail Markers as well as making the trail difficult to follow in many locations. Then too among the high mountain slopes avalanches had literally destroyed all trace of where the trail and the Spanish monuments marking the trail had once existed.

The first time Sebastian lost the trail he spent a week looking for the trail before giving up for two months as he simply felt that without the trail markers he could go no further. Later he had been following the trail through the eastern slopes of Taos Mountain when the hair stood up on the back of his neck and he simply froze for a minute. Then slowly and silently he moved back to his horse and removed the rifle from the scabbard (rifle holster). Slowly he cocked the hammer of his rifle. His senses screamed at him. Yet he knew not where the danger lay. Carefully he scanned the terrain. On his left side were the high steep cliffs. Yet he did not see hostile Indians there. In front of him he saw no threat. For there was a perfectly clear terrain, with only two hundred year old pine trees and fresh young growth on the ground. Behind him there was no danger just three large pine trees hundreds of years old. The terrain is perfectly flat and level and no one was hiding in the clearing behind him. To Sebastian's right side was a stream about four feet wide. The hair on the back of Sebastian's hair stood up warning him of danger. But as carefully as he looked he could perceive no threat. The only thing he saw on the far side of the stream was a stack of bare trees all carefully pruned to remove their branches and all the logs were stacked like match sticks on the other side of the stream.

Putting his horse between anyone hiding behind the logs and himself, Sebastian carefully advanced towards the logs with his rifle at the ready. Sebastian was prepared for danger. Yet after walking around the logs piled up like match sticks he realized he was alone. Sebastian was perplexed, for it would take a dozen men working a week with a team or two of mules to stack up the logs. Yet there were no axe marks on any of the trees. Turning from where he came from Sebastian looked towards the mountain and in a flash of sudden realization; he suddenly knew what had occurred here. A giant avalanche had come shooting down the steep mountain slopes uprooting the trees and stacking them like firewood on the other side of the creek.

Yet the same avalanche that had up rooted the trees and deposited them on the opposite side of the creek, had also destroyed every Spanish Marker and deposited the marker stones in a pile of rubble and stones beside the trees. The trail was gone. For a week Sebastian searched for the trail in the area of the avalanche, sadly Sebastian found no trace of the so he returned to his home in Taos.

One night, Sebastian awoke from a dream which he clearly remembered in every detail. In the dream he saw the Spaniards making trail monuments along the trail to the gold mine. Every step of the trail was well marked by them. Then as he rode his horse along the trail suddenly an avalanche roared down the mountain in front of him removing a portion of the trail. Yet in the distance he saw the trail on the other side of the avalanche and he saw him looking for the trail and finding it again and again tracking it closer to the mine. When Sebastian awoke from the dream he remembered it all clearly. He knew exactly where to look to continue following the trail. Yet the winter snows had come early. The snow fall had closed off the higher mountain slopes, so Sebastian would have to wait for next spring, after the snow melted to look for the trail again.

When Sebastian worked in the Archives back in Seville, locating the rich mine was something, he and his fellow archivist, literally the men whom were now his partners thought would take a week or two. And in another two weeks he envisioned he would be secretly loading up several mules with stacks of gold bars and headed back to Veracruz and catching the first Spanish Treasure Galleon back to Spain. Never did his partners or he conceive that in the first two years Sebastian would still be trying to work out the first league (2.18 miles) of the rugged trail to the mine he searched for. Doubt arose in his partners minds if Sebastian truly would keep his word and share the gold, and if he was really doing his best to locate the rich mine from which he was sent to recover the gold. Once a year a letter arrived in Spain detailing the royal trail markers Sebastian had discovered and his progress in following the trail as it wound counter clockwise up upon Taos Mountain.

Sometimes, as Sebastian worked his way up the mountain, he deliberately left the trail to hunt for elk and deer, whenever he encountered anyone else from the settlement of Taos up in the mountains gathering firewood or hunting. Sebastian always told anyone he saw he liked the solitude of the mountains and it was here he would find the best hunting. Never did Sebastian want the local Spaniards in Taos to suspect his real purpose was to locate a rich mine and secretly remove the gold. Occasionally Sebastian stopped in a cantina (bar) in Taos for a drink. Sebastian would listening to the conversation to learn about mines and mining but seldom did he speak or ask questions, as he did not want to draw attention to himself.

****

Jacquez DeShan had come over from France to make his fortune, trapping beaver, martin, bear, lynx and otter. While in Montréal, Canada Jacquez joined a group of Voyagers working for the Hudson Bay Company which had outpost across thousands of miles of the Canadian wilderness. The Voyagers explored the frontier and trapped beaver, martin, lynx and mink selling their furs to the Hudson Bay Co. Four hundred years later you can still find Hudson Bay Company stories all across Canada.

Jacquez had heard from other trappers that at Taos one could find a mill and distillery to the West at Arroyo Hondo. Here one could trade the furs for food, supplies like powder (Black powder-explosive to propel the lead bullets) and shot (lead bullets) for the muzzle loading rifles. You could buy new traps for catching beaver and other furbearers and most important of all there were Spanish Senoritas (women) and Taos White Lightning (whiskey). Jacquez had not been with a woman nor had he had any whiskey in a year. It was a situation he intended to fix in the spring after the snow melted and he had plenty of prime furs to trade.

So it came to pass that in May, Jaquez was headed south out of Colorado. He was headed south towards Taos along the west side of the Mosquito Range, the Front Range and the Sangre De Cristo Mountains following the centuries old Indian trade trail known as the "Rain Bow Trail" going through Costilla, Questa and heading through Arroyo Hondo to Taos.

At Arroyo Hondo Jacquez stopped at Turley's mill for a hot meal, real Indian bread from flour ground at the mill and what he wanted most some Taos White Lightning (whiskey). Jacquez met Simon Turley who had come out from Missouri to trade goods on the frontier. Liking the land and seeing the opportunity to finally buy some land and work on saving some money for his old age, Simon Turley first purchased some land to erect a house with sufficient farmland, and have irrigation water for his crops.

Then, Simon erected a mill to grind grain. His was the first mill in northern New Mexico. The mill was turned by irrigation water in the acequia (irrigation ditch). Then, when any one wanted their grain such as corn, wheat, oats ground into cracked grain for livestock or flour for making bread and tortillas, Simon would grind the grain to the required consistency in his mill. Cracked grain only had one or two passes through his mill, while high quality fine flour took several passes the grind stones. In return for grinding up the grain Simon Turley charged 20% of the grain he ground into flour. So if Simon Turley spent five hours grinding up corn into ten large bags of flour he would charge the farmer two bags of grain. This grain or flour would then be used to make bread or used in his still to make the mash for whiskey.

While Simon Turley helped many men by selling bread, gun powder, shot (lead balls-ammunition for the muzzle loading rifles, buying trapper's furs, selling whiskey he also made many enemies. Why did he make enemies? Simon could sell flour cheaper than any merchant in Taos so some store owners were angry that Simon took their business away by selling at a lower price. When Simon made whiskey he made a high quality product which took business away from the cantinas (saloons) in Taos. Farmers wanted to have their grain ground up but they got angry as he had lots of grain on hand as he ran his mill processing grain from many farms. When they left on their carreta (two-wheel ox-pulled cart), they left with their small load but they saw his mill had many bags of grain stored up from all the grain he processed. They often felt that since he was a rich man he should grind their grain for free.

Yet the three things that made the Hispanics and the Indians maddest of all was that first he was dating the Hispanic and Indian women as they considered him a good catch as a husband, this made many Indians and Hispanics jealous of him. Second he refused to give anyone (both Indians and Hispanics) whiskey unless they paid for it! And what angered them most of all was that this Anglo was obviously inferior to the noble Indian and Hispanics races. It infuriated them that this inferior white race expected to be treated as an equal when any one could instantly see he was of the inferior white race!

Don Blanco was furious when Simon Turley asked his daughter out. Who could imagine a bigger insult to his honor, than that an inferior white man, thought he should even be allowed to be in the presence of his daughter. Why his family had the Spanish blood of the Conquistadors running in his family blood line! Don Blanco's blood boiled at the insult!

Then in the fall when the harvest was made, Don Carlos had to take his grain to Turley's Mill to be ground into chicken feed for his chickens and a finer grind for the flour for bread. Don Carlos did not conceal his anger of Simon Turley very well. Don

Carlos was still extremely angry that a man of obviously and inferior race had insulted him by asking his permission to court (date) his daughter. Inferior races should know their place. Don Carlos anger extended to yelling at the men loading his cart, as he called them lazy gringos (insult-white person, like calling a Mexican a "wet back").

So, as the workers at the mill loaded up his carreta, they decided to have a little fun at Don Carlos' expense. After twenty identical bags of grain were ground up, Simon Turley let Don Carlos select sixteen bags of flour to be loaded into his cart. Because workers were Anglos and treated rudely by Don Carlos, they played two tricks on him. While loading the carreta one of the workers slipped two big rocks into one of Don Carlos bag of flour. Then as they finish and Don Carlos was about to drive off one worker said to the other worker in a deliberately loud voice so Don Carlos would easily hear them.

"You put all the bad flour with the worbles (bugs) in it in his cart didn't you?"

The other worker replied, "Of course, and in the underweight bag of flour I added some rocks to bring the weight up to the other bags."

Of course, all the bags were identical and held about forty pounds of flour. To prevent anyone from feeling they were cheated, Turley always let the customers select their bags of flour first. Yet when Don Carlos heard what the workers said, he was so furious, he took out his whip and angrily whipped his oxen into motion.

While Simon Turley always let the customer pick out his bags of flour first, this time the workers had added two large rocks to one bag to tease Don Carlos. When Carlos unloaded his flour at home his anger exploded. Instead of just flour, out of the top of one bag rolled two large stones! That Simon Turley was a thief and a crook. That gringo had deliberately filled his bags of grain with rocks. (There were only two rocks placed on top of one bag of flour—all the bags in fact had the correct and the same amount of flour).

In the cantina that night Don Carlos told everyone who would listen about how that thief and crook, Simon Turley had filled all his bags of flour with rocks!

****

Five years passed before Sebastian worked out the Spanish Trail to the lower Spanish Mines on the East side of the mountain about half way up. The good part of locating these mines was that it showed Sebastian that the stories about the early mining on the mountain were absolutely true. It also showed that Sebastian had learned reading and following the early trail markers with enough expertise that he could follow the trail all the way to the mine. Yet he felt that these mines were too exposed to work in secret as frequently he encountered wood gathers and hunters. If he was seen working the mine and it was reported to the authorities, then every time he left the mountains his mule packs would be searched and he knew there would be surprise searches of his house by the Spanish authorities. Getting the gold bullion out of Taos would then become impossible.

Yet it was the most intangible of all assets that San Sebastian took from locating the two mines that would in fact have the greatest impact upon his life. For in working out the trail to two Spanish mines San Sebastian took away with him the *confidence and self-assurance* that he could follow the trail and locate the Spanish mines where ever they were hidden as well as *perseverance* for he knew, if he had done it once, he could do it again!

It was while Sebastian was working out the trails that Jacquez first encountered Sebastian. Jacquez had frequently heard the story Sebastian told the in the cantinas, that he rode up into the high mountains to hunt. Yet as Jacquez watched from one side of a meadow as a dozen elk grazed on the lush green grass, Sebastian rode up into the meadow where there were numerous elk he could shoot for meat. Yet Sebastian never even removed the rifle from his rifle scabbard (holster) on the horse. Instead Sebastian was clearly looking at the rocks on the mountain slope above the meadow. For the rest of the day Jacquez simply followed Sebastian.

At first, Jacquez thought Sebastian was prospecting as he seemed only interested in rocks. After tracking Sebastian's movements for half a day, it appeared he was looking for faces in the stone, and he was going from one stone face to another as he traveled up the eastern slopes of Taos Mountain.

Jacquez noticed that most of the faces had an air hole beside the face and sometimes in the stone face itself. Clearly the stone faces Sebastian was following were manmade. It was on the third day as he tracked Sebastian, that he saw Sebastian remove a leather parchment or hide from his picket and as he repeatedly looked from the leather in his hands and they looked at the stone figure before him that Jaquez realized that Sebastian was not just following ancient stone faces but was in fact following a trail on a map marked with the stone faces. Jaquez may just be a poor French trapper, but he was not stupid. No Spaniard would spend years following a trail of stone faces on a map he carried unless it lead to something very valuable—like GOLD!

****

****Spanish Marker-A man's face—to get the exact direct to travel to the next Spanish marker simply look through the eye and it guides you to the next Spanish marker.****

Over a campfire that night, Jacquez thought of a peaceful way he could meet with Sebastian and clearly let him know he knew what he was doing, and he wanted to work with him. Sebastian only seemed to be able to track about two hundred yards of the trail in a day—as he constantly back tracked his trail and often covered hundreds of yards in width as he was trying to not miss any of the stone monuments indicated on his parchment or map. So Jacquez simply moved four hundred yards ahead of him in the direction he was traveling and located a Spanish Marker consisting of a stone face of a man with an air hole through the eye. Then Jacquez went and shot an elk and set up a camp with a fire to cook the meat and await Sebastian's arrival tomorrow evening.

The following evening Sebastian saw the campfire ahead of him and wondered what to do. Sebastian considered turning around and returning to his adobe in Taos as he did not want anyone to know what he was doing. On the other hand on this trip he had worked out almost four hundred yards of the trail, which was more that he had accomplished in the two years of work. He did not want to quit now. On the other hand he would like the companionship of another person for the night and a hot meal would be nice. From a hundred yards away Sebastian could smell the elk meat cooking over the coals of the fire. What harm could come from sharing a hot meal over a campfire, he thought.

In the fire light, Sebastian saw the fire was built below the stone face he was looking for. He smiled to himself, surely the French trapper was too stupid to realize the stone face was anything other than simply a natural stone formation.

Jacquez waved his hand motioning Sebastian to come in and join him at the fire and join him in sharing his supper. As he motioned the Spaniard over to his fire, he jokingly said in French: Salut, mon associé/Salut á mon partenaire (Hello, my partner).

And so over the course of time and many shared meals and campfires Sebastian and Jacquez did became partners and the best of friends. They traveled together in the mountains, hunted together, ate together, and worked together. They spent more time prospecting in the mountains together than they spent with their wives. And is this not true of many individuals today in the work place; they spend more time with their coworkers or business partners than with their wives or children?

Sometimes Sebastian went with Jacquez to Turley's Mill for White Lightning as they both occasionally popped the cork on a jug of whiskey. Holding the jug in the crock of their arms they would lift up their elbow tipping up the bottom of the jug of whiskey. Then the whiskey flowed out of the top of the whiskey jug, into their mouths. No one made better sipping whiskey in New Mexico than Simon Turley.

Neither Sebastian nor Jacquez were saints. Sometimes they went over to a cantina on the plaza in Taos and there they would exchange an elk quarter or furs for fifteen minutes of a woman's time. The first time Jacquez took Sebastian to such a room, Sebastian simply sat down on the bed, and talked to a young girl his daughter's age. All Sebastian could do, was talk with her. When he asked fifteen year old Angelina how she came to be here entertaining men for money, she told Sebastian that when she was fourteen years old, she had fallen into sin when the Taos padre had come to her parent's house and told her parents that he needed to instruct their daughter in the Bible. Receiving her parents' permission the padre took Angelina to his living quarters beside the church and throwing Angelina upon his bed, he promptly raped her. Every Sunday the padre took the daughter for Bible instruction and raped her repeatedly. Angelina was too ashamed of what was happening to her to say anything. When she finally told her father she was with child, he slapped her across the face and threw her out of the house and told her; do not ever come back.

"What was she supposed to do?" she asked. "I had no money, no food, no shelter, and no place to go. That is how I ended up here entertaining men and taking care of their needs for money. If you should talk to Ruth in the room across the hall, she too was repeatedly raped by the Taos padre and when she told the padre she was pregnant he told her she had three choices, to kill herself, to find a farm boy and tell him she wanted to marry him or go here to the cantina like all the prostitutes do. The padre told her if she would say he was the father of her child, then I will excommunicate your entire family and you will all go to hell."

The priest told Ruth that, "I am God's personal representative here on earth and I have been placed here by the Pope. I represent GOD, so if you defy me you are defying GOD himself. So if you do not want to suffer the wrath of God, you will go away now, and never speak of this again. If you should ever say I got you pregnant then I will surely bar your entire family from the gates of heaven!"

"What was I to do? Angelina asked.

Sebastian said nothing as he held Angelina in his arms as she cried, and tears fell on his face and shoulders.

When Sebastian left Angelina's room, he lied and told his friend Jacquez that he had enjoyed rolling and playing under the covers of the bed with Angelina for that is what he felt all men would say. Instead of having enjoyable and relaxing sex; Sebastian left the girls room with a feeling of outrage! He was angry that a son of a bitch like the Taos padre would take advantage of the young girls in his parish.

What was even worse, was that the very man the families and young girls trusted, breached that trust, and raped the young girls. Sebastian left the cantina that morning and he took with him an understanding of the Taos Padres real character. For Sebastian realized the priest, the respected man of the church, was simply a wolf in sheep's clothing preying upon young girls whom were very vulnerable and deliberately using his authority as a trusted padre to ruin many lives. Certainly the Taos priest lacked dignity, honor and integrity. Over the next few months

Sebastian heard many similar stories about priest of Taos, as he had raped over a dozen young virgins.

When Sebastian was home he had to look for Mary as she was often out gathering herbs. This activity scared Sebastian greatly as he prayed that the Commissioner of the Inquisition would not hear of such matters. Possibly the priest in charge of the Inquisition would not have time to examine such trivial matters, but one could never be too careful. For should one be arrested by the authorities, and brought before the Inquisition it was not a question of one's guilt or innocence, for you were always found guilty. It was just a matter of time before one broke under the interrogation as anyone having hot burning coals applied to one's bare skin or having nails driven into one's body, while being starved to death, was sure to confess any sins they were ordered to confess. Few people ever lived through the interrogations of the Inquisition. For once one confessed one's sins, then your property and assets were seized and you were then put to death.

When Mary turned thirteen years of age her beauty caught the attention of Taos priest of the Franciscan Order. The good Father came by Sebastian's house at dinner time. So Sebastian invited the padre to stay for dinner which had already been served and was in plates on the table. After supper the Taos priest admonished Sebastian for missing church on Sunday, and said how since Sebastian was away hunting in the mountains so often, that he considered it his duty as a man of the cloth, to instruct Sebastian's daughter Mary in the scriptures and prayers so that she would grow into an obedient wife for her future husband.

Sebastian immediately lost his temper and pulled a knife on the Taos padre. Sliding the hunting knife under Franciscan priest brown wool robe, Sebastian put the sharp knife blade up against the padre's penis and balls and said, if the padre really felt the need to instruct his daughter in the Holy Scriptures, he would do it without his man hood for he would cut it off first! Jacques smiled as he saw the terror upon the priest face. The Taos priest never forgot the insult and the threat made by Sebastian as Jacques smiled as he understood the priest worst fear. The priest swore he would see Jacques, Sebastian and his entire family in hell, even if he had to take him there himself.

From that day forward Sebastian and Jacques knew they had made an enemy for life of the Taos padre. Sebastian and Jacques tried to stay out of the padre's way when possible. They never again attended the Sunday mass the Taos priest gave. When the good father talked about the evils of Turley's Mill and how the gringos always were trying to cheat the Hispanics and Indians the padre always mentioned Sebastian and Jacques as part of the corrupting influence of the devil.

****

In Abiquiu, padre Manuel Gallegos also hated the dam gringos or "diablo's americanos" (devil

Americans). Whenever he had the opportunity to gossip and encourage anger between the Anglos and the Native Americans and Hispanics he did so. There was no gringo that Padre Gallegos did not feel would be a better gringo after he was murdered and the good father sent him on his way to hell. Padre Gallegos facilitated the meeting of men who lacked tolerance and understanding of their fellow men. Padre Gallegos of Abiquiu worked with men in Mora, Taos, Santa Fe and Las Vegas whom hated the Anglos as much as he did. Tomasity (Tomas Romero) of the Taos Pueblo and Pablo Montoya would lead the Rebellion to remove the hated gringos (white race) from all their land.

Padre Gallegos was simply a Catholic priest whom did not believe in tolerance for other races, religions, or skin colors, or national origins. He felt the best way to get along with the "diablo americanos" or "gingos" (racial insult-for a Caucasians) was to simply kill them where ever they could be found. At the Lady of Guadalupe Feast in Abiquiu on Dec 12, 1846 the padre proposed killing all the non-Indians and non-Hispanics found in New Mexico. One of the dates he proposed for the assassinations was Dec. 24. He wanted to get all the killing done before he held mass on Christmas Day celebrating peace on earth and the birth of Jesus.

****

After the visit by the good Father, Sebastian always took his daughter with him into the mountains.

Sebastian did not want his daughter to be raped, like the more trusting Hispanic fathers had allowed to occur. Fourteen years after having left Seville for the frontier of Nuevo Mexico, one still found San Sebastian and Jacques still searching for the lost gold mine. Now though San Sebastian was accompanied by his thirteen year old daughter Mary.

Mary was San Sebastian's precious daughter and so much more. Mary was the one person whom knew San Sebastian as no other. He kept no secret from her, he confided in his daughter even thoughts he would never speak of to his wife. Sebastian trusted no one else but Jacques and his daughter Mary with his treasure maps to the rich gold mine, and he taught her how to see and recognize the Spanish Trail markers. There was no secret, Mary did not know of her father.

When Mary had first begun tracking with her father, she had listened to him skeptically as he explained how the Spaniards made eagles and how one stood in front of the Eagle and then looked over the Eagles right wing tip for the direction to travel or the next Spanish marker. Mary was skeptical of his explanation and many of the stones he called eagles as they were simply a larger round stone representing the Eagles body and a stone to the left and right representing the wings. Three one hundred pound to five thousand pound boulders lying alongside a trail did not exactly look like a trail of Eagles and clearly marked trail directions to Mary.

Mary told her dad, "Are you sure it is not your imagination or so many years of wishful thinking, as you look for some imaginary gold mine?"

So her dad told her, "If they are random stones there will be no discernable trail or direction that they go. But if they are as I have taught you, then you will in fact see they travel in a specific direction and lead to another Eagle or Spanish Marker along the trail to the mines." Then her dad pointed out several Eagles on the trail ahead to his daughter. For ten more minutes as they walked Sebastian instructed his daughter about the compass stones which were thousand-pound flat stones held off the ground by smaller one to two foot round stones to that a large air gap could easily be seen under the compass stone. He then showed his daughter a compass stone and how one can look at the stone faces for the direction to travel or one can stand on top and look for a major crack running across the stones surface. The closest direction the crack ran towards one of the four major compass directions; north, east, south or west represented the way to travel. Sebastian showed his daughter a stone face as they traveled down the trail and how they had placed an air-gap authenticator to show that it was a Spanish Trail marker. He also showed her how when one sighted through the "eye" of the stone face it gave one the direction to follow.

Mary listened to her dad a few minutes more as he talked about the humor some of the Spaniards occasionally showed occasionally placing a Spanish marker on the left side of the trail then the next trail marker on the right side of the trail and they alternated which side of the trail where the marker was located. Without another word she looked up ahead and on the sky line she saw the three one ton boulders representing the body and the two wings of the eagle. Before her dad could catch up with her she faced the eagle and looked over the bird's right wing and took off in that direction.

That night they camped on the high northern portion of Taos Mountain. As they spent the night they built a fire to keep the cold nights air at bay. Around the campfire Sebastian complimented his daughter on her tracking skill. Never again would he be able to track as fast as his daughter as she had a natural born gift in tracking few possess.

The tracking had started at six in the morning without the benefit of breakfast. By eleven all Sebastian and Mary had on their mind was the hunger in their stomach after having spent five hours climbing up and down the mountains in the thin mountain air. So both walked back to camp and began gathering firewood to heat up the frijoles (beans) and tortillas (flat bread). Using the Indian method of a bow to rapidly spin a stick, a tiny ember was coaxed into a flame and shortly thereafter a small fire was used to heat up the beans. As the father and daughter ate lunch they discussed which areas of the mountain to search next.

Sebastian wanted to get moving so they could easily reach his favorite camp spot. There was a cold spring with an abundance of water as well as an abundance of dry firewood from a group of dead trees. There they would build a fire for cooking the beans and tortillas and have water to wash up as well as drink.

May ask her dad if he could just stay camped here a while longer as she had twisted her ankle and it hurt to walk. Reluctantly Sebastian agreed to his daughters request.

Yet as they ate they occasionally glanced up at the mountain slopes they had been climbing all morning. While there were no easily visible Spanish markers on the mountain slope at eleven am when they began building a fire; that certainly was not the case an hour later at noon. For Sebastian suddenly lowered his bean burrito to the ground and pointed up to the north face of Taos Mountain. Mary's eyes followed the pointing arm of her dad and there before them were a dozen Spanish markers using the sun's shadows to show the trail that they should follow to the mine site.

A easily visible stone heart had appeared as the suns shadow cast at noon created a ten-foot-tall heart. Below the heart four dots of rocks illuminated by sunlight guided one up to the stone heart. Then if one were to look over the largest and longest lobe of the heart there appeared to be a line of shadow wedges whose wedge points seemed to create a line going hundreds of feet further up the slope to guides one's path toward the hidden mine entrance. The wedges were shaped like splitting wedges with the pointed end at right angles to the path one was to follow. Sometimes there were two wedges created by the sun's shadow and the path to follow traveled between the points of the wedges. At other spots there was just a shadow wedge on the left or right side of the keeping one traveling in a straight line.

Two hundred feet to the east of the shadow wedges guiding one up the mountain slope was a twenty foot shadow bird facing the direction to travel. Out in front of the giant bird was a single straight line also created by the sun's shadow at noon. It appeared that further up the mountain slope that the bird trail might possibly intersect with the shadow wedge trail.

Lunch was forgotten as Mary and her dad walked West looking up at the mountain slope. As they traveled along the mountain slope suddenly a cluster of rocks which they had walked by a half a dozen times and it had never caught their attention had a hole carved in solid rock shaped like a giant church bell. When they looked through the opening having a bell shape they suddenly saw two giant boulders with the top two feet lite up by sunlight while the lower portion of the mountain slope at this location as still dark and in shadows. The bottom center of the bell opening where the clapper was, lined up in a perfect straight line with the two stones higher up the slope whose top two feet came to a point and this was catching the noon day sun light.

A hundred vara's (approximately 95 yards—a vara is 32 inches and a common unit of measure centuries ago) further west was a giant fifteen ton three leaf clover. What this symbol meant or how it was used neither Mary or her dad knew. Both realized that somehow this huge stone three leaf clover was intended to take them up the slope of the mountain before them.

Another hundred yards further walking found them moving counterclockwise towards the south west as they moved around the northern slope of Taos Mountain. Here they saw a giant flat stone divided in half by a shelf a foot high. The line created by the two levels of the stone seemed to point up the mountain slope towards the general location that all the other lines were heading. Having his daughter Mary stand on the giant flat stone he had her guide him up the mountain slope in the direction the straight line showed them to travel. Whenever her dad wandered too far to the left or right of the straight line Mary shouted to her dad to move to the left or right as needed to keep in a straight line. As Sebastian moved up and climbed the mountain slope he was suddenly faced with a giant boulder with a "V" notch made right in the center of the stone boulder. About another hundred yards further up the slope Sebastian came to two eight foot tall boulders leaning together. The center where both boulders rested against each other again formed a "V" notch.

Looking down the mountain slope towards his daughter, Sebastian realized the "V" notches lined up perfectly to where his daughter stood in the distance.

The flat boulder with the line or shelf running across it lined up perfectly with the "V" notches of the boulders higher up on the mountain and were designed to guide one up to the mine site. Slowly Sebastian realized that the early Spanish miners had created a series of different markers all going to the same location in case one set of markers was destroyed then other sets of Spanish markers would still lead one to the concealed mine entrance.

Suddenly San Sebastian burst out laughing. He could hardly control his laughter as he realized what had really occurred in the last few minutes and what the real lesson was. His daughter had known about the boulders and the "V" notches all the time and that they were simply seeing another method of following the trail to the mine. But instead of telling her dad, or showing off her tracking ability his daughter had sent her dad up the slope to learn another method of tracking the way to the mine. His daughter had stood on the bottom flat stone and guided him straight up the slope so he would deliberately run into one Spanish marker stone after another.

Wave after wave of laughter rolled over Sebastian and he had to hold his stomach as he suddenly plopped down on the ground beside the huge "V" notch boulder. Sebastian had spent over a dozen years looking for this mine and suddenly as he thought back to their lunch. Suddenly it had occurred to him that his daughter had suggested they stop early and fix lunch so they were in the exact position to see the stone heart and the shadow wedges.

Sebastian continued to laugh as he thought back to when he had wanted to push on to a regular camp site he liked and his daughter and said she was simply too tired to go further and her ankle was hurting from all the walking. As he looked down the slope he realized he had forgotten about her story she fed him last night about her sore ankle. He had seen no evidence of a sore ankle that his daughter complained of hours earlier and she had been climbing up rough rocky ridges for five hours. She had known the location of the mine all along! She had just been discretely getting her dad into a position where he would discover the Spanish markers and realize how to read their meaning.

Sebastian rushed up the slope to the concealed mine's entrance but instead of a black hole or a mine door Sebastian saw nothing. Several times he hurried down the hill to a Spanish marker set only to rush back up the hill again to find nothing. Finally Sebastian listened to his daughter's advice and extended a number of white rocks in a straight line. By evening Sebastian had two straight lines extended up the mountain slope. Working all the next day' even skipping lunch Sebastian, Jacquez and Mary were able to extend three more lines up the mountain slope. Over dinner they excitedly talked over their discovery that all five of the lines intersected within a half of vara (16") circle!

The next day as they explored the site further they located two more lines using "U" notches leading to the same location. One set or series of points consisted of right side up "U" notches set in arranged stones. The second set of "U" notches they located was the same except the "U" notches were upside down like they were representing a mine tunnel ("n"). They knew it could not be an accident or coincidence that all seven lines led to the exact same location.

As Sebastian, Jacquez and Mary walked over the site where all the lines intersected one thing was clearly obvious to all. There was no indication they could see on the ground marking the location. It simply looked like all the surrounding mountains. Nothing would draw your attention to the correct spot to dig. There was simply no trace that a rich gold mine existed at this location. After carefully studying the location so that they could easily return to this exact site, Sebastian, Jacquez and Mary mounted their horses and headed for Turley's Mill. At Turley's Mill in Arroyo Hondo they planned to obtain shovels, picks, a digging bar and a hot meal. Before leaving they would also buy some food to last them the next couple of days until they had time to dig out their treasure.

Three days later, one would again find all three treasure hunters back at their mine site, high on the north slope of Taos Mountain, where they began digging. Approximately every twenty minutes the digger took a break and traded places so a new rested individual was digging. That evening three exhausted prospectors sat around the campfire and talked excited about what they expected to recover tomorrow.

They had pushed the hole down five feet, and in the morning they expected to deepen the hole another foot or two. Once they were down about one estado, (old Spanish unit of measure = 5'7") then they expected to find the stone entrance to the treasure room. Over the camp fire Sebastian talked about his partners back in Spain whom had entrusted him to find and recover the treasure, he was sure that they had about given up on his recovering a treasure. Sebastian talked about the look of surprise they would have when he returned to Madrid, Spain with a mule load of gold bars.

Sebastian was a man of his word; and he would keep his word to his friends. Though many years had passed he envisioned the difference this money would make in helping his partners live out their old age. Instead of poverty and depending on relatives to give them a meal they would be able to own their own house. They would have servants to serve them hot delicious food and they need never worry about where they would find the money to buy food for dinner. If they ever became sick, they would be able to afford the best medical care. One man, he remembered, said he would buy a small four vara (11') fishing boat so he and his family could have fresh fish for dinner.

Jacquez thought back to his family he had not seen in thirty years since he had boarded a small sailing ship in La Havre, France for Canada. He had never until this campfire discussion ever envisioned his seeing his family again. Tears streamed down his face as he talked of seeing his mother and father. Jacquez turned away from the campfire and wiped the tears from his face, as up until now, he never considered he would have the opportunity to see his family again. His father and mother would be so proud of him. He would buy some land and build them a nice house. Jacquez wondered if the pretty neighbor girl was still single. In Veracruz, Mexico they would all be able to get passage aboard a Spanish treasure galleon to Spain. From Spain Jacquez would be able to work his way north across Europe to his birth place in France to see his family again.

A modern replica of what a Spanish Treasure Galleon looks like. This one is available for boat rides at Port Isabel, Texas at Pirates Landing.

Mary was so happy she could help her dad. She wondered if indeed she would see the great city of Madrid her dad had spoken of so often, and if she could attend the University of Madrid. She had always wanted to see the places her dad spoke of, as well as the giant treasure galleons which sailed across the seas. Mary wanted to see if truly there were seas a thousand times bigger than the Rio Grande upon which one traveled for months and never saw land. Possibly her dad occasionally told tall tales, for how could a river ever be so big? Mary thought her mom would want a fine house, dresses and servants.

They awoke at daybreak. The fire was out and a wind blew from the southwest. A weather change was in the air. No one fixed breakfast. Like an unspoken understanding they all went directly for the hole. Jacquez started digging.

After a foot of dirt was removed, he was helped out of the hole by Mary. Then Mary's dad began digging at the bottom of the hole. The dirt he threw out of the hole was removed by Mary as she shoveled the loose soil and rocks away from the edge of the hole to prevent it from falling back into the hole and to make it easier for the digger so they did not have to throw the dirt over the pile of dirt.

As Mary watched her dad dig, his pace gradually quickened as he uncovered the top of a rounded arch of a stone door way. Jacquez noticed the interest Mary showed looking into the hole, and he too moved closer to look into the hole. As Jacquez saw the rounded arch and the beginning outline of the door take shape, he told Sebastian to come out of the hole. Sebastian you look tired and anyway it is my turn to dig. Sebastian climbed out of the hole with an excitement in his step. Jaquez climbed into the hole and excitedly he threw a shovel full of dirt into Mary and Sebastian's face.

Mary said, "Watch it, please."

Jacquez replied, "Excusez moi, s'il vous plait."

Sebastian and Mary moved further back as the dirt flew in all directions. After Jacquez had deepened the hole two feet further, Sebastian said it is my turn now. With another two feet of digging there was a five foot high mine or tunnel entrance. They then attacked the door way and the stacked rocks blocking the door way fell into the tunnel.

Jacquez dropped his shovel and raced into the tunnel, Sebastian helped his daughter Mary down into the hold and he slid in behind her knocking her down in his hast to look too. Helping Mary up, they rushed into the tunnel behind Jacquez. About ten feet into the tunnel Jacquez stood staring at am old Spanish knight in a suit of armor.

The knight looked like he had just sat down with his back against the wall and his legs outstretched. He had on the metal helmet the Spanish knights wore in pictures and he wore a steel breast plate which seemed to have turned dark with rust from moisture in the mine.

As they looked at the knight in armor, one could see his death was caused by a wooden spear sticking out of the front of his metal breast plate. As they approached closer they could see the metal point of the spear had exited out the back of the dead Spaniard! Beside the Spaniard was another dead Spaniard stretched out dead on the floor. Beside and covering his body were two bags of high grade gold ore.

Fist-sized chunks of gold ore lay about the dead Spaniard. Wire gold was easily seen in the rusty red quartz rocks. In places it seemed the gold was almost the width of one's finger in the rocks. Mary noticed she was having trouble breathing. Her dad seemed not to be getting enough air.

Suddenly Jacquez said, "We must leave now. The air is bad."

Grabbing the two leather bags, they moved the ten feet to the door. At the doorway, Mary scrambled out into their freshly dug hole. Behind her, Jacquez threw one leather bag, scattering its contents out of the bag and throughout their hole. Her dad just threw his bag, hitting her and knocking her to her knees as he crawled into the hole in his haste to escape the mine tunnel. Jacquez helped Sebastian as they both staggered out of the hole.

Upon reaching the outside of the hole, they revived in the fresh air. Over the next fifteen minutes they said little, mostly simply breathing and throwing the high-grade gold ore out of the hole they had dug down to the mine entrance and onto the ground above them. They all realized it had been a close call. If they had not left the mine when they did, they would have died due to the bad air.

Sebastian said, "We will have to enlarge our hole a little before leaving to allow fresh air into the mine. We will have to air out the mine."

Jacquez said, "I think we will give it a week. For now, we will load up this gold ore and take it to Turley's Mill. He will help us crush it and extract the gold. I know that Simon Turley told me he ships his placer gold back to his brother in Saint Louis, Missouri."

Sebastian said, "For now we will load up these two bags of gold ore and take them with us. While Mary keeps watch we will bury it at Turley's Mill in the horse corral. We do not want anyone is to see us doing business with Simon Turley."

Two hours later, they were riding for Turley's Mill. Everyone was in a good mood as their dreams they had spoken of around the campfire would now become a reality.

Arriving at Turley's Mill on January 19, 1847 they arrived at ten at night. An old trapper was doing guard duty, leaning back against the stockade gate smoking a clay pipe. When building his mill, distillery and trading post Simon Turley had enclosed it all behind a wooden stockade. There was even a corral for the horses, and some housing for visitors spending the night all protected by a wooden stockade.

Leading the horses into the corral, they carried out their plan of burying the high-grade gold ore as planned while Mary kept watch. They then pushed the horses over the site where they buried the high-grade gold ore. The horses were used to remove any trace that they buried a treasure in the corral. Now they all felt much safer. Then they went into the mill for to find a quiet place to sleep. In the morning they would discuss their business with Simon Turley.

****

Juan Blanko was listing to the Taos priest church sermon denouncing the evils of the devil, and the devil's seed now living there among us at Simon Turley's mill. The good father spoke of the evils of whiskey, and how the dam gringos were stealing their grain, their land. They were infidels who were Christians and Protestants, not good Catholics like them, who worshiped the true God. Then Juan Blanko jumped up and shouted out how they wanted to steal their daughters, and how he had taken his corn there to be ground into grain and instead of the bags of corn they gave him they just gave him bags of rocks.

Outside in the plaza, on the morning of January 19, 1847, Pablo Montoya rallied his supporters and told them we must drive the gringos out of our land now he shouted. Pablo Montoya shouted above the crowd's roar, get your guns or any weapons you have now and we will send these dam gringos back to hell where they came from. In ten minutes there was a large crowd in front of the Ranchos de Taos church and this large mass of men headed for the Taos Plaza.

At the Taos Pueblo, Tomasity (Tomas Romero) rallied the Pueblo Indians to join him to kill the gringos. Hundreds of pueblo Indians grabbed their bows and arrows and knives and followed him towards the Plaza in Taos where the two groups combined and joined forces. Along the way more and more Indians and Hispanics joined the crowd. The men carried rifles and bows and arrows, wooden clubs, knives and shovels.

Pablo Montoya and Tomasity led the mob from the plaza. Leading the mob, they intended to kill every Anglo and representative of the American government that they encountered. Going one block to the north to Bent Street the mob headed straight for the dam gringo governor.

When Governor Charles Bent came out of his house to calm the crowd they promptly shot the governor full of arrows as they had no intention of talking. Then pulling out their knives they scalped Charles Bent in front of his wife and children. Pablo Jaramillo, Charles Bent's son-in-law was murdered next. They had come to kill every gringo (white man) they could find!

Stephen Lee the Taos county sheriff tried to stop the mob, but he was no match for the hundreds of armed men whom murdered him on the south side of the plaza.

Next, the mob killed Cornelio Vigil the county judge and JW Leal, an attorney. Judge Beaubien son hid in an outhouse. A Hispanic servant of the family ran out to the mob and told them where they could find a gringo to kill. The judge's son Narciso (Narcisse), was found by the mob, and promptly murdered.

The following day, January 20, 1847 Montoya and Tomasity rallied hundreds of supporters to finish the job and kill the gringos at Turley's Mill. As the crown moved out of Taos towards Turley's Mill in Arroyo Hondo, it steadily increased in size as hundreds of men joined in to kill the gringos and steal whatever they could. By the time the mob reached Turleys mill there were over five hundred men intent upon murder.

From the mill and distillery is started as a quiet day, the men had just finished breakfast when they received warning from Charles Autobees that an angry mob of about five hundred men was now heading straight for them! Hundreds of Indians and Hispanics were advancing for them and it looked and sounded like they wanted blood.

Simon asked Charles Autobees to ride to Santa Fe help. Simon Turley took charge and ordered his men to close the gates and the mountain men started molding lead bullets over their coals from the breakfast fire. It looked like the wild mob intended to kill them all.

Simon Turley was offered safe passage if he handed over all the other men in his mill to the mob so they could be murdered. As a man or honor and integrity, Simon stood by his friends. He would not turn them over to the mob to be slaughtered.

Soon the mill was surrounded and the battle started. The rushes were initially repulsed but the defenders felt that their best chance to live was to try and escape at dark. Men on both sides died in the fighting. Many of the men inside the stockade were mountain men and trappers so their bullets began to kill the members of the mob whom tried to storm the gates and open them up to allow the mob's entry into the mill compound. When the mountain men's accurate shooting drove them back they encouraged the Indians to use their bows and arrows to shoot burning arrows into the stockade.

Since most of Turley's mill, the distillery, the housing, the barn and stockade wells were of logs the entire structure quickly caught fire. Once the mill was in flames, it no longer protected the men behind the walls. Quickly, the structure became a burning trap. When the first men tried to run out the gate they were quickly cut down by the mob and killed.

Sebastian, Jaquez, Mary, Simon Turley and six of the surviving mountain men mounted their horses. In a wild rush they would all make their rush together out the front gate upon their horses. Sebastian buried two brothers beneath a pile of horse manure, they chose to try and hide rather than fight their way through the angry mob intent upon their murder.

Later during the night of the second day, these two men managed to escape. The ruthless attack by the mob so terrorized these two brothers they never were like their former selves. The attack left their mark on these two men so they never were able to recover after the senseless murder of their friends.

Out the gate they rode in a wild rush, firing their guns into the angry mob. While the angry mob was intent upon slaughtering everyone leaving Turley's Mill, when their horses were killed, they fought in a small circle as the mob rushed in and killed them all. Sebastian died fighting to save his partner Jaquez and his daughter as they tried to escape the angry mob.

The only Anglo rider to escape the mob was Simon Turley. By some fluke of luck he was able to ride through the mob. As he looked back he saw his entire life's work up in flames, his friends dead and he wondered how he alone had escaped alive. Then his horse collapsed out from under him, dying from a half a dozen arrows. Simon Turley was then alone, on foot, walking north on the Rainbow Trade Trail towards San Crustibal. As he walked north he encountered a Hispanic man, Senior Gonzales, whom many times he had traded supplies with in his store and whose grain he had ground into flour. Simon handed the man his gold watch and asked him to get him a horse.

The Hispanic man, Senor Gonzales, then told him he would be happy to help an old friend, and to wait right there for him, and he would return within two hours with a horse. Then senior Gonzales walked south to Arroyo Honda where the angry crowd had completely destroyed the mill and killed the men and women inside. Outside the mill the mob was stealing all the loot they could. The cattle, pigs, goats and chickens of Simon Turley were being gathered up by the mob of Mexicans and Indians and divided amongst themselves.

Senor Gonzales carefully weighted his options, as he saw the large crowd of Indians and Hispanics. He could keep his word and bring Simon Turley a horse and help out his friend in his time of need or he could enjoy a greater momentary reward and esteem in the eyes of the ruthless mob, by telling the crowd where to find Simon Turley so they could kill him. Clearly this was the best choice of all, he could keep the gold watch, he did not have to give his friend a horse, and surely Simon Turley would not complain after he was dead. So senior Gonzales proudly led the mob to Simon Turley and they promptly murdered him!

As the sun set the mob returned to their homes. The Taos padre, was caught up in a dilemma of his desire to be rid of his enemies, yet this belief conflicted with his desire to offer shelter and help those in need. In the end, Taos padre sheltered about twenty men who sought his safety. These were family members of those killed by the mob. Yet the padre also sought pardons for those involved in the killing.

He also got to see the mutilated bodies of Sebastian, his daughter and that French fur trapper Jaquez. The padre smiled as he realized that in one day he had eliminated his three most hated enemies, without lifting a finger. Truly it was an act of GOD. Even his enemies Simon Turley and Governor Bent died. Yes this was a really great day. God would be really proud of him for this day's work. All about him were those dead Protestants and Christians. The Taos padre knew in his heart that God only truly loved the truly devoted Catholics like himself!

From the ridge-top, Senor Blanko looked down upon the dying embers of the ruins of Turley's Mill. Senor Blanko realized that he had sure shown Simon Turley and all those Rocky Mountain and Hudson Bay fur trappers their proper place in hell. Who did that dam gringo Simon Turley think he was anyway? Wanting to go out with Senor Blanko's daughter! Why his daughter could trace her ancestry back to Spain. He was just some no account, white man whom did not know his place. Well he had put him in his place today! Why the king of Spain would probably want to pin a metal upon him or knight him for killing all those Americans who had come into New Mexico.

When senor Blanco walked through the ruins and among the bodies of the dead, there beside Sebastian and the Fur trapper was a fist-sized chunk of high grade gold ore. Senor Blanco's anger exploded. If only they had lived long enough to tell him where they got the gold. He could have gotten them to confess if he had only twenty minutes alone with them. Next time, he vowed, he would not be so quick to kill. This looked like the gold from his families lost mine somewhere up there on Taos Mountain. Now they (the three dead prospectors) took the secret; it went to the grave with them. Senor Blanko screamed in frustration. He wanted that gold.

Among the dead, beside their charges were thirty two Angels of the Lord. They wept and cried at the senseless slaughter brought upon these men and women, by men's: intolerance, hate, greed and prejudice. Where was man's love for his fellow man (or woman)? Where was man's humanity and love for his fellow man? Where was the dignity, the honor, the integrity? The Angles cried over the men and woman that they had done their best to watch over in this life time.

Suddenly, from out of the dead bodies, there arose the spirits of the dead men and women. To the north of the massacre site there appeared a golden door with an Angel of God upon each side of the door. All the angels encouraged the Spirits to enter the door of brilliant white light. Some spirits simply got up to fight with the spirits they had died trying to kill in their previous life time. They simply refused to let in the light of peace, joy, love, tolerance, respect and understanding of unconditional love of the Angels. Half the Spirits moved with the Angels toward the wonderful white light.

Sebastian looked down at his dead body, then beside him he saw an Angel. Glancing to his left he saw his daughter's spirit also standing beside another Angel whose wings glowed in the sun set. Then he saw his friend Jacquez's spirit with a third Angel beside him. Together the three friends walked with the Angels beside them into the white light. About half the spirits who died chose the path of the Angels and walked into the light. Behind them two Angels guarding the gates to heaven followed them into the tunnel of "White Light." Instantly, the light was gone. Half the spirits, those remaining at the massacre site, continued their fight, feeding off their energy of anger, prejudice and hatred of individuals of a different skin color. God would not, the Angels would not, force them to change, for God had given them *free will.*

So should you go to Turley's Mill today, where the ruins are—you will still find many angry spirits or ghost. God gave them free choice, and their choice at present is to retain the anger and hatred of people of different races and skin color. What about you? What will your choice be? God has given you free choice, too.

****

About two weeks later, law and order returned to Taos. Of the hundreds of men involved in killing the governor Bent, and killing the men and women at Turley's Mill only twenty nine were arrested and tried. Twenty nine men, both Indians and Hispanics were found guilty and ordered hung by the neck until dead.

The Taos padre felt it was his duty as a Franciscan priest to comfort these men in their time of need and crisis. Each man felt the comforting words of the good padre as he explained to them the way the political systems work. The padre told each man if he would deed over to the padre his house and lands that the padre would use the money to bribe the judge and secure their freedom. Once the men signed over the deeds to their property to the Taos priest, the Padre immediately went to the court house and recorded all twenty nine land deeds in his name.

Then the padre took a trip to Abiquiu to visit with that parish and preach before the congregation. The Taos padre met with his good friend Padre Gallegos. Padre Gallegos was keeping a low profile as he did not want to be associated with the ring leaders of the failed revolt.

When the men who were sentenced to be hung sent word to the Taos padre that they needed help immediately, for they were to be hung shortly, the padre simply ignored their pleas for help. On the appointed days of the execution, all twenty-nine of the men were hung.

Then the padre left Abiquiu and returned home to Taos. With a smile on his face, the good Father looked over his lands and smiled, for surely now he was the richest man in Taos. If only he had a more responsible position in the church, the padre thought, he could have done some real good. The padre's only regret was, think how many more teenage girls he could have taught the scriptures of Jesus to, and how much more land he could have acquired, if he had been an archbishop.

When Pablo Montoya and Thomas Romero (Tomasita) died, they immediately had two choices. Their spirits saw before them the door to heaven with the Angels guarding each side of the door of light. In the distance they saw the ruins of Turley's Mill, and they realized that this to them was really their finest hour as they slaughtered their enemies. The two Angels did not block the men from the gate to heaven; it was their desire to continue their hate and killing which drew them back to the mill at Arroyo Hondo and to this day that is where they reside. GOD gave both men free will, but like a double edge sword, it cuts both ways; they can move towards GOD's love and grace or away from it.

****

In a green mountain valley beside a stream of crystal cold stream, three Guardian Angels sat down beside Sebastian, Mary and Jaquez. They talked about the life lessons each of them had chosen. They had chosen as their life plan to work with lessons of: friendship, dignity, honor and integrity. For even in their deaths they had shown they had learned and practiced these lessons until they ceased to exist on the physical plane. On the spirit plane where they now sat beside the Angels, they would always exist in GOD's eternal love. As they discussed the lessons they had learned and the lessons they chosen as their next "life plan" they smiled as they realized they had progressed one step closer to GOD.

****

So tell me, when you sit down with your Guardian Angel and discuss your life plan, how are you coming along? Are you learning the lessons you have chosen to learn? Are you helping those you can in their time of need? Are you treating your spouse, your children and those around you with dignity, honor and integrity? When you have an extra fifty dollars in your wallet have you used it to help the least of God's children-those hungry and in need?

Of course you can always turn your back on those less fortunate and in need. GOD has given you *free will. If you do not like (your) the life lessons, you are experiencing in your life right now so well; I hope you realize you will come back and repeat them, time after time, until you get your life lessons right! With free will it is your choice. So choose wisely, or one to two centuries from now you may be experiencing the exact same lessons and events in your life that you are experiencing now!*

The Angels sat silent and watched
For they knew what was to unfold
Lessons would be learned
Trails would be tracked
And secrets long concealed, would be revealed
And GODS grace would flow all around and about

The Magic Carpet Ride

To the west of the old coal mining town of Trinidad, Colorado is a small log studio and it was here that Molly O'Brian came to spend some time with her daughter Briana. Like a lot of children Briana had a mind of her own and did not always like her mother telling her what she needed to do.

When Molly told Briana that it was time for her afternoon nap, Briana told Molly, "First you have to read me a story."

Molly told Briana, "Go to the book shelf and pick a story you want me to read to you."

So Briana walked over to the book shelf and selected a well-worn book called *PATH OF THE ANGELS*, which she opened to a short story called: "The Magic Carpet Ride."

"Briana," Molly said; "Why don't you pick another story, I have read you that story at least a hundred times."

Briana replied, "I do not care. I like the story because the woman has the same name as you do mommy."

"Ok," Molly replied, "but next time I want you to select another story."

Getting comfortable on a couch, Briana lays on the couch with her head facing her mom as their feet touch under the blue fleece blanket. Their heads are at opposite ends of the couch as they face each other. Molly picks up the book and begins to read the story her daughter has selected.

The Magic Carpet Ride

Molly O'Brian has left the mountain range of Canada del Oro, north of Tucson, as she was uncomfortable tracking the trail that Dancing Wind had selected. For this trail had great danger, dangerous lions and many dead upon the trail. Molly chose not to track the trail any further after encountering a Spanish death trap which almost took her life and did in fact bury her backpack costing her $2,000 in camping and prospecting equipment. Molly knew she would never forget the lesson she experienced and she would never forget that appearance of the death trap which had buried her pulse induction metal detector. After encountering the remains of a Mexican tracker whom had died in a Spanish death trap in the shape of a stone heart, with tears in her eyes, Molly told Dancing

Wind that this certainly was not a trail of her choosing and she would not go any further.

So Molly decided to leave Arizona and go visit and stay awhile with some friends in Espanola, New Mexico. Espanola is a small Hispanic town along the Rio Grande and is known for its "low rider cars" and its pretty women. Molly would spend her days driving to Santa Fe where she would visit the Palace of the Governors and then swing by the Spanish Archives where she would conduct her research.

One evening Molly stopped by the Sonic drive-in for a hamburger, coke and banana split. Four teenage boys walked by her and looked her once over. Then one of the teenagers commented loudly to his friend: "She would be an "8" if she was not so chubby. I guess I will rate her as a 2."

The insult about her weight cut into Molly's heart like a knife. Why she wondered did the teenagers have to be so cruel? Molly had been doing her best to try to watch her weight. The banana split was the first dessert she had eaten in a month. Molly thought people should not be less reckless with their tongues. Never should you make fun of another individual, deliberately hurt another's feelings, or slander another's reputations. Never should one use your words recklessly like a knife, to hurt another.

That night as Molly said her prayers she resolved to lose fifteen pounds this year. She decided to lose two pounds a month. The following day, Molly took off and traveled south to go see Dan. Dan was an older

Lakota Indian, a medicine man, a very good friend, but really so much more. Dan had taught Molly not only tracking but about many aspects of life.

Dan was truly an elde,r with white long hair running down his back in two brads. His face could be kind or show the fierceness of a warrior which he truly was. Dan's actions always showed dignity, honor and integrity. He had also given her some basic instruction on using a hand gun for self-defense. Yet this visit was to ask Dan for his advice on the best way for Molly to lose fifteen pounds.

Dan told Molly, "You will lose the weight; if that is a choice you choose to make. Yet choosing to lose the weight is just the first step. You also have to take action to implement the weight loss. For to achieve any worthwhile goal, it takes thought followed by effective action."

Dan suggested Molly take daily bicycle rides up into the mountains of the Santa Fe National Forest. Besides, he told her, "I think the rides will relax you and you will enjoy the beauty of nature and the wildlife on your rides." He added with a grin, "Who knows what else you may find there, as you ride your bicycle through the mountains."

Molly looked at him with curiosity but Dan added nothing more.

The following day found Molly looking at the bicycles at Target and Wal-Mart. Molly wanted a nice bicycle with baskets to carry her lunch and her supplies she normally carried like a few bottles of water, an air pump, a rain coat, a map of the area she was riding, a compass, GPS (global positioning system), spare batteries, sunscreen and a Glock for self-defense. Neither store had baskets on their bicycles so she decided she would have to buy those separately. She wanted a comfortable wide seat and she also had to decide if she wanted a steel Huffy bike or an aluminum Alex bike which was lighter. The Schwinn bikes had gears which can make peddling the bike easier. Then she also wanted some lights on her bike for safety. There was more to selecting a bike than she thought.

Molly selected a Huffy bike for its low cost. Then she modified the bike by adding the headlight and a flashing LED taillight. And two baskets' on each side of the rear wheel and a front basket attached to the handle bars. In the bike tire tubes she added the green slime to prevent flats from thorns. Then in red paint she carefully painted the name of her bicycle on the rear fender. Molly called her bike *"The Magic Carpet Ride."* Now she was ready to ride.

Packing a lunch, Molly was off for an afternoon ride. Leaving Espanola behind her she rode to the west. Past the New Mexico State Police station she rode her bicycle. As she peddled her bike to the west the road before her changed from pavement to gravel as she left Espanola behind. The first days ride took her to where the forest road 144 began to climb the mountain at the base of Clara Peak. Here her energy gave out as the mountain grade quickly steepened, and she was huffing and puffing until she could go no further.

Turning around and riding back to Espanola she was proud of herself for she had ridden 17 miles.

The following day Molly rode the same route again only this time she rode two hundred yards further up the mountains road. Each day that passed she got a little further up the hill. By mid-September Molly was riding all the way up to the top of the mountains and then she cruised miles beyond, on the forest service road 144. In October Molly began taking along a tent and sleeping bag as she explored further and further into the Santa Fe National Forest.

The forest consisted of green aspen trees, juniper, and tall reddish orange bark ponderosa pine. Sometimes Molly surprised elk feeding in the greener patches of grass which grew alongside. Usually she saw the female elk as they seemed much more plentiful than the males (bulls) with their larger antler spreads. Sometimes cotton tail rabbits and the taller long legged jack rabbit caught her attention. Because she rode her bicycle, its silence enabled her to silently slip up and encounter the rabbits and elk. Occasionally Molly rode by small herds of elk which had not heard her silent approach.

Sometimes, Molly would set up her tent in a meadow and fall asleep under the stars. During the night she sometimes awoke and would hear and smell the elk feeding in the meadow around her. Molly knew that if she smelled the elk, they were within twenty to thirty feet of her sleeping bag. To see the elk feeding was one of nature's delights. Some nights she removed her night vision gear to more clearly see the elk feeding. Some nights there would be a dozen elk in sight and other times their might be several dozen as the night vision scope showed her many elk in the greenish glow.

As the months passed, the hills became easier to climb and her rides became longer. Molly's stamina and endurance increased as her body weight slowly decreased. She missed her dear friend and teacher Dan, and she wondered how Dancing Wind was doing tracking in the Catalina Mountains north of Tucson. Molly felt that her time was growing short in Espanola and she felt change was blowing on the westerly winds.

Molly had heard stories that Dancing Wind and Dan told about the Abiquiu Priest Arturio, whom worked in the mountains to the south or southwest of the old pueblo of Abiquiu and while she knew that Arturio had returned to Heaven to be in GOD's hands she felt that if Dan and Dancing Wind could recognize Arturio's camps then maybe she could also recognize where he camped. So, over the past several months Molly had kept her eyes and heart open as she kept an eye out for the ancient camps of the holy man.

It is a spiritual truth that what is constantly on your mind will be attracted to you. This is true whether your thoughts are of love or anger, compassion or indifference, harmony with the environment or disharmonic actions. For whatever your thoughts are of, they are in fact creative, creating either good or bad experiences in your life. And so too were the thoughts that crossed Molly's mind about the man of dignity, honor and integrity—the priest Arturio.

It was in the third week of October, in the Fall Season, when the frost was in the air, the nights were turning colder and the Aspin trees were shedding their yellow and brown leaves that a fast moving storm came out of Arizona and swept into the high mountains of the Santa Fe National Forest. Suddenly Molly was engulfed in the thunder storm.

First came the hard gust of wind. Suddenly the tall green pine trees were swaying as the wind swirled all around her. Slowly the large drops of rain began to fall about her. Molly saw the individual drops of rain as they splashed onto the light brown road, suddenly turning it into dark brown as the dirt becomes wet with moisture.

Suddenly Molly was engulfed in sheets of hard driving rain. In just a few moments she was soaked to the skin and the temperature cools down twenty degrees. Lightning crackled across the sky as well as bolts of lightning slammed into the mountains around her. It seemed like there is a high electrical charge in the atmosphere, almost like static electricity.

Molly continued riding as she looked for some shelter. Rainwater seemed to come in sheets, with each gust of wind. Rainwater ran down her face. Her clothes, saturated with water, stuck to her skin. Lightning bolts were followed by roaring claps of thunder. Waves of raindrops seemed to skip and sweep across the road, as if dancing on the wind. The full force of the storm was now upon the mountains where Molly rode her bike.

As Molly rode down the dirt road, she looked for any place she could find shelter from the storm. Suddenly she slammed on her brakes and came to a complete stop in the middle of the road. Dropping her feet to the ground to keep from falling over she stared in amazement at the far side of the meadow in the edge of the trees. Never before has Molly seen such an unusual sight as she now witnesses on the opposite side of the meadow.

There, on the opposite side of the meadow, she saw a cluster of large five and ten foot tall boulders. There among a group of half a dozen boulders, she saw a shimmering white light, a golden light, and two blue lights shimmering above the ground through the heavy rain fall. As Molly looked on in amazement the shimmering lights are changing shape and intensity yet they stay over the same location of the ground. Suddenly Molly remembered her camera she carried, packed in the rear saddle basket.

Doing her best to shield and protect the camera from the driving rain by leaning forward and placing the camera under her jacket front she walked her bike off the road and began to slowly advance upon the shimmering lights. Stopping every five or ten paces, Molly snaps several pictures of the shimmering lights. Molly carefully looked for a cause of the lights, but there is no person anywhere within sight. What or whom is causing the lights she has no idea.

Cautiously, Molly moved closer and closer as she took picture after picture until she was about twenty feet from the shimmering lights. Molly then moved clockwise around the lights and the boulders in a circular manner, as she snapped picture after picture.

Some of her pictures captured the white light; some of her pictures captured the blue lights and some of her pictures capture and recorded the gold light. For there, among the half-dozen huge boulders, were four shimmering lights, seeming to come out of the ground. One light was shimmering gold, a second was shimmering white, the third and the forth glowing lights shimmered a royal blue. Molly smiled for she had captured them all with her digital camera.

Water ran down her sleeves; her face had water running down it and water dripped off her nose. Her wet hair was soaking wet in the driving rain. Her clothes were so wet that anyone could wring water out of them. Even inside her tennis shoes, she could feel the water squeaking as she walked. Literally Molly was as wet as if she had fallen into a river and emerged crawling up the wet slippery banks. Yet Molly was as happy as could be, for she knew she had dozens of unusual and unique pictures.

Tired, cold and muddy from one fall she took while riding on her bicycle, Molly peddled back to Espanola. Upon arriving home she peeled off her soaking wet clothes and dropped them on the bathroom floor as she stepped into a hot shower.

Molly just relaxed under the hot water running over her body. Nothing could dampen her excited mood. God, she felt she had a wonderful day.

Putting on a thick white cotton Turkish bathrobe Molly put a tea kettle on the stove to boil. Getting a tea cup off the shelf, Molly added two large spoonsful of honey and a peppermint tea bag to her cup. As the water boiled Molly filled her cup with the steaming water and took her cup to the study. Turning on her computer she waited for it to start up and ask for her password. Typing in her password, Molly then inserted the SD chip from her camera into the side of her lap top computer. Then she opened the photo file. For a few moments nothing happened and then her first picture appeared on her screen. She smiled as she saw the wet grass and dirt of the meadow and the rear of her bike. For in her excitement she had snapped a picture as she removed the camera from the rear basket.

One hundred and ninety pictures followed, each one getting closer and closer to the shimmering lights. The pictures began at a distance barely showing the lights on the far side of the meadow until the last ninety pictures showed the white, gold and blue lights from a distance of ten to twenty feet as she photographed them at dozens of different distances and angles as she moved around the shimmering lights.

Selecting ten of her very best photos, she E-mailed them to her beloved spiritual teacher, to explain the phenomena she had experienced. Then she phoned Dan to ask him about the pictures and what was causing the glowing lights and why they were different colors.

Dan asked Molly, "Were there any Spirits there?"

"I did not see any," Molly replied.

Dan said, "I asked you if there were any spirits there?"

"Just a minute," Molly replied. Then she asked GOD to put a White Light of Protection around her. Then she turned to her Guardian Angel for her advice and counsel. Molly asked her Guardian Angel if there were any Spirits there around the site with the glowing lights?

Her Guardian Angel told her, "No."

Then she asked her Angel if she failed to see any of the spirits that were near the site?

And again her Guardian Angel told her, "No."

Then she asked her guardian Angel, "Is there was any danger at the site?"

This time, Molly's Guardian Angel replied, "Not really; as long as other people do not see what you are doing, then there is no real danger."

So then Dan replied, "You have accessed the danger and there is very little, as long as other people do not see you at the site. You have ruled out the lights being caused by spirits or ghost. That leaves the possibility then that the storm altered the atmosphere by putting an electrical or ion charge in the air and combined with the moisture the glowing light appeared. The important question of course is, what is there that caused the lights to appear in only four locations." Dan then said, "Possibly you have photographed *treasure lights.* Why don't you check them out when the weather clears. Who knows," he told her, "you just might find a nice surprise waiting there for you."

Two days later, Molly peddled her bike west along forest road 144. She had taken her tent sleeping bag, backpack, four MRE's (meals ready to eat) and a pick, a 17-pound digging bar and a shovel. In her backpack were half a dozen pictures of the exact location of the shimmering lights. Since she did not have a metal detector she would use the pictures to show her the exact spot to dig.

Three hours after leaving Espanola, Molly arrived at the boulders on the edge of the meadow where she had photographed the glowing lights. The top photo in her backpack had a white light, so that was the location Molly selected to dig first. Molly first tried the shovel but the shovel would not do more than scratch the hard dirt surface. Taking the digging bar Molly loosened up the first three inches of soil. This she removed with the shovel. Then she resumed breaking up the soil and again removed another three inches of dirt. Carefully checking the dirt she had removed she saw no trace of anything of value. So Molly resumed digging beginning with the digging bar and then using a shovel to remove the loosened dirt and rocks. Again at twelve inches she double checked the soil she had removed.

Again she shammed the digging bar into the soil listening it up for its removal. On the third blow of the digging bar she heard metal. Immediately she stopped. Grabbing the pick she used the pick end to scrap away the dirt careful not to damage her metal object.

Lifting it out of the hole, Molly observed the rusted remains of a metal knife. The wooden handle was gone. The knife left chunks of rusted metal that had fallen off the knife in the hole. Removing the knife from its resting spot Molly dug another foot and nothing more was seen or heard. The white light had indicated the presence of the iron knife. Refilling the hole, Molly thanked the Creator for the gift and mixed wild grass seed into the dirt as she refilled the hole.

Going to the second picture in her pile of photos, Molly carefully looked at the site of the blue shimmering light. Looking from the photo to the ground, Molly found the exact position where she saw the blue lights and she scuffed into the dirt its outline with her shoe.

Putting her photo aside, Molly began loosening the soil and rocks with her digging bar and then removing the loose soil and rocks with the shovel. Repeating the process every three inches the hole slowly got deeper and wider as Molly dug. Finally, at three feet, she again heard the sound of metal. So she widened the hole further so as not to damage the metal object, yet even so she heard the metal on metal sound as she used her pick to widen the hole.

Getting out a small trowel Molly worked to remove the dirt and rock yet not damage the metal object. As she removed more dirt she could clearly see a black metal bar. Lifting it from the hole she could feel the heavy weight of the metal bar and Molly realized she held an old Spanish bar of silver. Over the centuries that the silver bar had been buried the shiny silver color had been covered by a black tarnish.

A smile came across her face only to be replaced by a wide grin as she removed one after another metal bar of silver bullion from the hole. When she was finished Molly had six small finger bars of Spanish silver on the ground beside her! Taking her shovel she refilled her hole until it was within six inches of the grounds surface. Then she removed some Hopi Pink corn and planted it into the hole and continued refilling the hole so it was completely refilled. Then Molly said a prayer thanking God for his bounty and taking wonderful care of her.

Next, Molly stopped to take a break and eat lunch. Reaching for a MRE, she opened it and smiled in surprise for she found she was having a turkey snack stick, apple sauce, raisins and tortilla chips which she dipped into a cheddar cheese dip. From her canteen, she drank water.

The third and fourth photos were of a new location at the same site which also had a blue shimmering royal blue light. Here Molly repeated the same process of outlining the location to dig. Then she loosened the soil with the digging bar and removed the loosened dirt and rocks with her shovel. The only difference she observed between this hole and the other holes was at this site she was encountering charcoal and ashes like she was digging in the fire pit.

This time at two feet she discovered two small black finger bars of silver bullion. The silver bars were about one inch wide, one inch high and about twelve inches long. Again Molly refilled the hole and this time she planted several garlic bulbs in the loosened soil. Again Molly gave thanks to God for watching over her needs and providing for her so generously.

It was late afternoon when Molly removed the photos showing the exact location of the golden light. For two hours she dug her hole, getting it down to three feet deep. Yet she encountered nothing. Molly was so tired. She stopped and set up her tent and placed her sleeping bag inside. Then she gathered wood for a small fire. Mostly the fire was to keep herself company as she was all alone. By the fire she placed a cup of hot water for tea. Then she pulled a MRE out of her backpack and thanked GOD for a wonderful and interesting day and she thanked GOD for her food.

Molly opened her MRE and settled down to a meal of sliced salami, wheat crackers upon which she spread gruyere cheese spread, a pasta and vegetable salad, dried apricots, and a energy drink she made by mixing the energy drink with some water from her canteen in a stainless steel mess cup.

For an hour, as the fire burned down to reddish coals, Molly watched the fire and thought of her life, where she was going and what she would do with this gift God had given her. She knew she could not keep it all for it would show she was greedy and selfish and cut her off from GOD's abundance. So Molly would use a quarter to help those in need. Another quarter would be paid in refining and selling the silver. Yet Molly knew that even four bars of silver represented many thousands of dollars.

Maybe the time had come for her to look for some land. She wondered what land along the Purgatory River cost. Who knows maybe GOD was providing her with a place of her own. As the cold air filled the night and the temperature dropped down into the thirties Molly sat on her sleeping bag and said her prayers, to the *Spirit Whom Moves Through All things.* Soon Molly crawled into her sleeping bag and was fast asleep.

****(The Dream)****

Molly sat around the campfire and was sharing some beans and water with the priest.

The priest told Molly, "I have been expecting you. Did you know that you are at one of my overnight camps when I traveled to Espanola from Sierra De Las Minas? The silver you have dug up is not for you! I want you to change it into money and use it for charity. Every action you take to use the money must be to put, *Humanity back into human actions!* The silver was stolen by thieves from my mine. I expect you to spend every peso, as I have instructed."

Molly nodded to the priest and said, "You are a man of honor and integrity, so I will do as you ask."

Then the priest got up from the fire and started to walk away to the northwest. After walking about five paces he stopped and turned to Molly and said, "My friend, I hope you choose wisely in your actions of putting humanity back in the human experience. Certainly I have made mistakes, but I think I have not made one here tonight. When you dig in the morning do not stop until you reach one foot for each letter in my name. Arturio = 7' deep. When you dig at the golden light remember my words to you and I hope the gold buys you a nice piece of land, a house and a good horse."

The priest waved, and turned and walked away into the night.

****

Molly awoke from her dream inside her sleeping bag. She was positive she had been awakened by the hooting of an owl. Looking outside her tent the fire was out and there was no one around her camp. Molly remembered her dream and wrote down her dream in her journal, then she turned and crawled back into her sleeping bag. Burr it sure is a cold night.

In the morning Molly built a small fire to heat up some tea. Then she ate some cheddar cheese and crackers. Reaching for her MRE she shook the contents out onto her lap. Opening the applesauce she ate it next. Then she reached down for the cookies and jam spread. Squeezing out the jam she spread it on top of her cookies which she ate one after another. Then she used her finger to catch some jam running down her chin and licked off her finger with her tongue. As she drank her mint tea she recalled her dream which had awakened her during the middle of the night. Molly believed in the importance of her dreams and used them for guidance in her life.

Throughout the day Molly dug her hole deeper and deeper. In the morning when she began digging, her hole was at three feet as she had dug that far the day before. After four feet she would have quit digging except for her dream. At five feet her arms were so sore she could barely lift the digging bar. Sometimes the dirt she threw out of the hole was blown by the wind back into her face, and down her arms and down the neck of her shirt. The sweat mixed with the dirt blowing back upon her created a muddy dirty teenager. The dirt was getting in her hair, her face and even her eyes.

At six feet the hole was over her head. Already she had passed the depth the king of Spain required their treasures to be buried. Never would Molly have dug an inch deeper than six feet except for her dream. Yet deeper Molly dug, until she could barely lift the digging bar any more. Finally after seven hours of digging she hit seven feet. Carefully she then dug with a thick wooden pine branch scraping the soil away. In the center of her hole she found the treasure Arturio had spoken of which would provide her with land, a house and a horse. For before her was a shiny golden finger bar of gold Arturio had buried over a century earlier.

Taking the gold bar out of the hole, Molly began refilling her hole. It was ironic that a hole which had taken seven hours of back breaking sweat and labor to dig could be refilled in less than an hour. As Molly refilled the last six inches of dirt she mixed red clover with the dirt so it would grow in the spring.

Like an old-timer, Molly moved slowly, breaking camp and packing all her gear. Molly felt so exhausted. The eight silver bars went into the bottom of her blue backpack. The gold bar was wrapped inside of her dirty shirt she had worn yesterday. With all here gear packed Molly poured half of her drinking water on the site of the ashes of her morning fire. No smoke arose from the ashes, for they were in fact completely cold. Then walking her bicycle to the dirt road Molly got on her bike and rode out of the mountains heading east for Espanola.

As darkness descended upon the mountains, the Angels watched a teenage girl riding to the east. She had five red flashing lights on the rear of her bicycle and two white headlights lighting the road in front of her. Beside the Angels stood a priest, watching her leave the Santa Fe National Forest. As the priest watched her go, he thought to himself, "that looks like fun." So he hopped onto the rear baskets as the bike coasted down the hill by the forest service lookout tower. Molly never felt a thing as the priest rode along with her on her bicycle, for Spirits don't hardly weigh anything.

As Molly rode into Espanola, she turned south and rode along Paseo de Onate until she saw the Black Angus Burger. Here she parked her bicycle by the door and walked in to get a burger and chocolate milkshake.

As Molly exhaustedly begin to eat her dinner, one woman commented loudly for all the restaurant to hear. "Look at that woman, you can tell she is a witch with her red hair and dirty looks. She is going to hell!"

Another father looked over at Molly and told his son, "See what happens when you use drugs; it wipes you all out and you look like hell!"

A third person saw her bike and the letters written on the rear fender, *The Magic Carpet Ride.* Turning to his girlfriend he said, "I knew she was a drug addict. Flying carpet my ass, look at her. She is all messed up on drugs."

Molly just wanted to slide under the table and disappear. Outside the Black Angus Burger an old diesel pickup drove up to the restaurant. Dan walked into Black Angus Burger restaurant and ordered a cup of coffee. Then he walked over and sat down opposite Molly.

Leaning over to whisper in her ear, Dan said, "You look beat kid, can I drive you home?"

Molly replied, "I would love that Dan." Dan finished drinking his coffee as Molly finished her dinner.

Walking outside, Dan lifted the bicycle into the back of his truck. Turning to Molly, Dan said, "It seems you have a little extra weight here."

One old man saw Dan lifting Molly's bike into the pickup truck bed and thought that Dan had come to take his runaway daughter home. Both Dan and Molly realized that many different people had observed them in the restaurant and all had reached widely different conclusions of what was occurring, and all the conclusions were wrong. None of the conclusions were correct but people like to gossip.

Five days later, in Phoenix, Arizona, Dan and Molly exchanged the gold and silver for cash. The money from the eight bars of silver went to a shelter for battered women. The sale of the single gold bar enabled Molly to purchase her first piece of land as well as a small log studio in Colorado.

****

Molly put away the story she was reading her daughter. Her daughter Briana was fast asleep.

When Briana awoke two hours later she told her mom, "Let's go for a bike ride."

As they got on their bikes and peddled down the road, Briana turned to Molly and said: "Your bike has the same name on it as my favorite story." In faded red paint on Molly's old bicycle on the rear fender was painted: *"The Magic Carpet Ride"*

The Angel came bearing a warning:
"Do not cross the mountains in the morning
For ice lay under the snow
And if you insist you must cross the dangerous pass
An accident you will surely have and a
A hospital you will surely all go!"

Sarah's Life Lesson

The sun rose in the east across the Sangre de Cristo Mountains. Sara greeted the rising sun in her prayers as she prayed along the Rio Grande Gorge in the Wild Rivers Recreational Area. Below her in the bottom of the gorge flowed the muddy brown water of the Rio Grande River on its way to the Gulf of Mexico.

Beside Sarah a Lakota Medicine man also prayed. Dan had the weathered look of a man who had witnesses many seasons come and pass over many years. His gray and white hair hung over his shoulders in twin braids. The years had added many lines to his sun darkened face. As he prayed he asked the Great Spirit to watch over Sarah. Dan prayed for his student's safe return and that Sarah would survive the lessons she would soon be faced with. For The Great Spirit had warned Dan of the danger she faced. For Sarah was playing with the forbidden fruit: a handsome man who lacked both honor and integrity.

****6 months earlier****

Sarah's husband had decided to replace Sarah with a younger woman. All Sarah's husband wanted when he left was all the money in the checking account, the savings account, the money from the sale of their stocks and the house. Sarah's husband Sammy had announced he wanted a divorce. Of course for the two previous months he had been selling off thirty seven thousand dollars of their joint stocks on the Dow Jones Industrial Stock Market. Their joint savings bank account of nine thousand dollars had disappeared and when Sarah asked Sammy about where all their money had gone he replied he had borrowed some money for his business from Sam McGill and now that he had sold some stocks and had a little extra in savings he had paid off the debts they had. Never during their marriage had Sammy said they were in debt and he was borrowing money from his best friend. Sammy's transactions had the smell of rotten fish or an outright lie.

Suddenly in the last few months, all their joint savings were suddenly disappearing. Literally all her husband had taken was everything! After Sarah's husband had left and the divorce was finalized, Sarah had met James at a dinner party. James was almost everything Sarah thought she desired in the perfect husband. James was polite, courteous, and ever so handsome; he took her breath away. He was very intelligent and had an in depth understand of finance, the stock market, commodity markets, and tax law. His only flaw, in Sarah's mind was that James had no desire to work. Sarah simply could not afford the thousand dollars a week it cost her to maintain James. Sarah wanted James to come back, but he had left her when her bank account had reached a zero balance. God, Sarah thought I want him back; if only James would get a job and go work. I know I can change him, she thought.

As Sarah cried at night she thought her whole world was falling apart around her. Sarah had been dumped by her husband and then by her ... what should she call him, she wondered? Her lover? Sarah had accumulated four weeks' vacation time so she decided to take three weeks off work. She needed time to think and pull herself together.

Nine days later found Sarah at the Rio Grande Wild Rivers Recreational Area located west of Taos, New Mexico. Why she came here, she was not sure. Was it the post card of the Rio Grande Gorge she saw in Albuquerque, or was there another reason she came to this remote corner in the American South West?

At the Bureau of Land Management (BLM) in Taos she learned of the campsites by the Rio Grande Gorge. Late in the afternoon she purchased some groceries and she drove out to find a campsite. Nightfall found Sarah camped on the east side of the gorge with the cliffs falling away hundreds of feet to the Rio Grande which flowed on south to Mexico. Here above the Stage

Coach hot springs she had set up a tent. At dark she crawled into her sleeping bag and cried herself to sleep. The wind came from the south west and heard her tears, they read her mind and the Wind Spirits felt her desperation and her cry for help. And so her prayers of help and pleas of desperation were carried upon the wind by the Wind Spirits.

She awoke on the tenth day of her vacation to the sound of an old Indian medicine man praying at daybreak. The smell of incense and sweet grass arose from the medicine circle. What prompted her to slip into her blue jeans and sweater and walk over barefoot to sit inside the medicine wheel, she never knew. The medicine man continued with his prayers. She listened for a while as her mind replayed the last few months' events over and over. Could she have handled it differently? Certainly she did not know how.

GOD how had it come to this. For twelve years she thought they were a happily married couple. She knew they had their occasional differences. Didn't every one? She thought she was a happily married woman until her world was suddenly shattered into a million pieces. Sarah started crying; how stupid she felt. Tears streamed down her cheeks and she started sobbing. Everyone knew about her husbands' infidelity except her. Why is the wife always the last to know?

Dan came out of his meditation to see a nice looking woman in her thirties sitting cross legged facing him inside his medicine wheel sobbing uncontrollably as tears ran down her face. There were individuals that tried to talk to Dan whom found that after twenty minutes of trying to speak to the medicine man got up and left, as he never acknowledged their presence, or acted like he had heard a single word that he had said. For if the individual lacked honor, integrity, or was just evil or mean the medicine man simply had no desire to associate with them in any manner.

Dan was silent a few moments as he spoke (communicated) with the woman's Guardian Angel. Then Dan took a few moments to consider if he chose to travel down this trail of tears. Then Dan smiled at his own humor. For Dan had thought, why does this woman chose men by their looks and charm instead of by their honor and integrity? Why don't people listen to the guidance of their Angels? Then Dan had smiled as he thought, most men in fact do the exact same thing (pick women by their looks and charm). Yet that is why both men and women are here on earth; to learn their life lessons. For Earth is a place where spirits come to learn and experience the lessons they have created. When one has learned and thoroughly understands one's life lessons then there is no need to return to Earth, to live one life time, after another life time, as one repeatedly tries to get one's life lessons down correctly.

Sadly, Dan looked into her past relationship with her last husband and Sarah's desire to have a relationship with James. Sadly he saw Sarah jumping from the skillet into the fire. Sometimes people are so stupid, he thought. Unfortunately she did not seem to see that there was little difference between her first husband and her new boyfriend, James. The only difference between her first husband whose behavior was like a shark, was her new boyfriend James was very much like an Alligator. They both ruthlessly destroyed whomever they worked with. There was really little difference between them. Both men were utterly ruthless and simply lacked dignity, honor, and integrity. They would lie, cheat, steal and yes, even kill to get whatever they desired.

James was a man who was only interested in a woman for her assets. The assets James was most interested in was not a woman's beauty or sexual appeal; James considered himself much more mature than that; his interest in a female was her bottom, her financial bottom line, literally the assets he could loot during the course of their relationship. James had already located another target to take advantage of and shake out of the money she had inherited from her parents. In thirty to ninety days, if everything went as planned, he would have power of attorney on her accounts and a week later he would leave, with all her assets. That he would leave his intended victim penny less was just their tough luck, as far as James was concerned.

He had married Jackie, to insure her trust in him. Then while she was at work, he was also working on her computer systemically working on cleaning out her stock portfolio. He had used the house key she had given him to let his friends in to strip the house of all the furniture while he was working at the country club lining up another woman whom had the type of assets he liked to take advantage of.

To ensure his business associates had plenty of time to strip the house bare he talked Jackie to meeting him after work for dinner. Then, when they arrived home, he expressed shock and outrage at the bold action of the thieves who had stripped Jackie's house down to the bare wood floors. In false anger he called the police and berated them for never being there when you need them. When pulled out his wallet and peeled off five one-hundred-dollar bills and handed them to Jackie.

He told her, "I know this does not make up for your loss but maybe it will help you a little."

Jackie was touched by James desire to help. She was so lucky to have found a responsible and loving man who would stand by her in her time of need.

The next day, when Jackie was at work, James stopped by and picked up his cut from the sale of Jackie's furniture. Though his partners only got about twenty cents on the dollar, James' share came to two thousand dollars. He could afford to give Jackie five hundred dollars of his cut from robbing her house.

Before he was finished, Jackie would never forget him. After he emptied her bank accounts and sold her stocks he would invite Jackie for a vacation in Mexico. He had suggested a beautiful four-star hotel with a wonderful view of Acapulco Bay and the beautiful sandy beaches. There he would even sell her car before leaving her stuck for the entire cost of the vacation in Acapulco, Mexico. When James told Jackie, he would take her on a vacation "she would never forget," he literally spoke the truth.

Jackie had even been kind enough to buy him a motorcycle. When she was in the shower he had removed her VISA credit card from her purse and ordered the Harley Davison motorcycle on line. Since he held her credit card he was able to provide his wife's three letter pin number on the back of her credit card. It did not raise any suspicion when he had it sent to her home address. She would not know it was a gift from her until he was long gone.

He had ordered the Harley Davison in two easy payments of twelve thousand dollars each. The first payment was covered by Jackie's available credit line of $35,000. The second charge which would occur while they were vacationing in Mexico, and would max out her line of credit. The remaining payment and her bill on her credit card would come after he was long gone.

While James was giving Jackie a honeymoon vacation in Mexico that she would never forget, he arranged for his friends who had burglarized her house to be there to pick up his motorcycle. They had the shipper's phone number to arrange delivery. Thanks to credit cards, most women had more money than they knew. And James was always willing to help out a woman, if she picked up the tab. And James never picked up the tab unless he was just setting the woman up to completely clean her out.

James never worked a day in his life; his old man had worked all his life and he just had a truck and a small camper he lived in. James was handsome, and he knew it, and he used it to seduce women. First, he got them to trust him. Then he got them out of their clothes. Next he cleaned them out of their money. Then he moved on to the next wealthy woman who made eye contact with him and could not take her eyes off him.

****

Sarah met James at a dinner party. James was simply assessing Sarah if she had any money worth his time to take. Within two evenings James got Sarah to open up and tell all. James knew Sarah's net worth was less than three thousand dollars. She owed more on her car than it was worth. She did not own the apartment she rented. Sammy, whom she had just divorced, had left her with the attorney bills to pay. Sammy had taken the stocks and the "T" bills (Treasury Bills) prior to leaving. Listening to Sarah talk, he realized she never saw it coming. She never recognized the signs, as Sammy liquidated the assets and hid the money away, beyond his wife's grasp. When Sammy sold off his boat and his hobbies stuff, and purchased ten thousand dollars in traveler's checks, James knew Sammy was just days away from leaving. James recognized all the signs, as he recognized the pattern he used when he cleaned out a woman and stole all her assets.

To Sarah, James was a handsome man, kind and considerate of her problems. The attention he gave her as she discussed her finances just showed his maturity. He actually listened to her; and asked intelligent questions. Oh GOD, why could she have not met James twelve years ago, instead of wasting twelve years putting up with Sammy. She could not remember the last time Sammy ever sat down and talked with her and listen to what she had to say. James brought flowers, a dozen red roses when he stopped by. She could not remember the last time Sammy purchased anything, other than something for himself.

Then, on Friday night, they went out to dinner and a dance. Sarah danced a dance or two with James and then he asked her to bring him a drink from the bar. She went to get a drink, and when she returned with James' drink, she saw him dancing with another woman.

Sarah told herself, "It's ok, I am not a jealous woman. I am a mature adult, James can dance one dance with someone else who must have asked him to dance." When she looked up again, she thought she saw them walking out the door together. Though she knew she was mistaken, he would not walk out on her without saying a word. It just had to be a mistake. Yet it was no mistake, he had abandoned her at the dance, without even leaving her a way home.

****

Sarah wiped the tears from her eyes. The old Indian who had been praying inside the medicine circle had suddenly opened his eyes and was looking at her. He smiled and held out his hand to shake her hand.

"Call me Dan. Would you like to join me for breakfast? You look hungry."

And so began the adventure of Dan and Sarah. To Sarah it was not an easy trip. Learning matters of the spirit was something for those do-gooders who went to church every Sunday; then failed to apply what was taught the rest of the week. Sarah certainly did not go to church every Sunday.

To Dan it was not easy to teach one who ignored his wisdom and had to be unnecessarily hurt. Yet, like a teacher and student, their relationship grew into a friendship that not only lasted a lifetime, but went far beyond our physical limitations and understanding. You might say that the relationship began over a prayer, or over breakfast. An Angel might take a different view point and say it had all been arranged - - - - the meeting - - - - had been arranged by the Guardian Angels. For the meeting was really about the Angels working with Dan to help Sarah, begin the process of opening up and interacting and communicating with her own Guardian Angels.

For it is in the process of doing good, of opening your heart, of acts of kindness and acts of charity as well as helping and interacting with nature that one opens oneself up to the Christ Consciousness and the Guardian Angels. As Dayna Mata says,

Sarah returned to work in Seattle, yet when she had weekends off she often combined it with two days of vacation time to make it a four day weekend and she would fly out and spend the time with Dan. Dan would teach Sarah about using medical plants for healing and they would also go for long walks in the Sangre De Cristo Mountains.

Along the creeks as they walked and talked Dan pointed out the green stinging needle which he picked and placed in a bag. Later he would cook these for dinner after boiling them and changing the water twice. Once cooked, they tasted like spinach. From the banks of the stream in the shallow water grew the watercress which tasted like radish. After washing it off it was added to their bean burritos.

During these walks they spoke of current events in the news, the economy, the wild animals they encountered, tracking, spiritual concepts as they applied to her life and the problems or difficulties Sarah had in her job. They also spoke of Sarah's recent life lessons, her former husband Sammy and her newer love James who had suddenly left her at a dance without even saying a word to her.

Dan wondered as he listen to Sarah describe her three-day affair with James if she realized how truly ruthless and dangerous he actually was. Dan tried to explain that James was like an alligator or a wolf hiding under a fur coat of a sheep he had just killed. He would attack and destroy anyone whom he considered vulnerable and having any assets worth his time to steal. The truth, when told to someone before a person is ready to listen, is like water washing off the back of a duck; it does not have much effect.

One day, Sarah and Dan went for a drive up into Antonito, Colorado in Dan's old diesel pickup. Initially Dan had suggested they go backpacking for five to seven days, but when they saw the old-fashioned coal-burning steam train, Sarah suggested that they go for a ride on the train. Dan suggested that they bring their back packs along in case they saw a nice location to backpack, then they could get off the train and go backpacking in the Cumbres Mountains.

When the train stopped at Osha Station, Sarah and Dan had a lunch prepared by the railroad and served in the cafeteria there. When they finished eating and the train loaded up to depart, one train going to Chama and the second train returning to Antonio, Sarah and Dan shouldered their back packs and went hiking in the mountains.

Within two hours Dan was explaining the basic concepts of tracking the Old Spanish Trails to Sarah. Then as they were hiking several hours later, they crossed the trails of elk so they practiced tracking the elk trail for three hours. When a coyote tracks crossed the elk trail then Dan asked Sarah to track the coyote trail and tell him where the coyote was going and what he was eating.

The next day they tracked a rabbit half the day, as Dan pointed out the feeding habits of different animals and the tracks they left in the soil. Several times during their tracking lessons they walked up within a fifty yards of grazing elk. They were in no hurry, so they investigated or explored whatever caught their interest. The conversations also bounced from one topic to another as Sarah asked questions that came to mind or Dan asked questions to explore a topic under discussion further.

On the third day, Dan again had Sarah return to tracking the Old Spanish Trail. These Spanish Trails led to old Spanish camp sites and the concealed Spanish mines located in the mountains they were exploring. He wanted her to be able to easily follow the monumented trail to the camp sites, water holes, mine sites and cache sites.

On the fourth day, they tracked a trail directly up to an old Spanish mine site. The fifth day was spent tracking the entrance markers, showing the exact entrance location to enter the mine tunnel. These are difficult to locate, as hundreds of years earlier the mine entrance had been cleverly concealed so that no one other than the Spanish could reenter their mine.

For seven days they walked through the mountains. While they walked for miles every day, the distance from Osha Station was never more than twelve miles distant as the crow flies. Twice they walked up to Spanish Mine sites. For by following the ancient Spanish markers, they had literally tracked the Spanish trail directly up to the concealed mine entrances.

Here, Dan pointed out several of the different death traps the Spaniards had placed centuries ago, to protect their rich gold and silver mines. Then, after he pointed out four of the traps, he insisted that Sarah point out an additional four traps to him. He showed Sarah how they placed the stone maps and then they carefully removed one map to read before replacing it in exactly the same position, location and direction as they had found it.

Spanish stone maps are positioned in the ground with true north aligning with true north on a modern GPS (Global Positioning system). So a stone map must never be moved until north is marked on the stone or you will lose the correct alignment of the stone map. Then they practiced tracking the centuries old trail to the front of the mine where the entrance was located. Then they practiced tracking to the back door or pozo. Both of these trails (the front entrance and the Pozo) are difficult to track as they have been carefully concealed a century or two ago.

Here, at one of the mine sites, Dan suggested to Sarah that she use his metal detector to see if she could locate any possible buried valuables like ore, silver or gold that may have been left behind.

First Dan showed Sarah how to use the pulse induction metal detector, then using the fifteen inch round search coil he suggested she search the camp. To help Sarah out he suggested she grid the camp up onto grids in her mind. Then search each grid. Dan then sat down on the grassy ground under a piñon tree (pine tree) and smoked his pipe.

The basic philosophy the wise old Indian was teaching to Sarah was, *"how to fish for her supper."*

Dan felt that if a person knew how to go out and catch fish, then the person would learn to feed themselves. If he gave you a fish, it was wrong as it encouraged the person to become dependent on you for the next fish or the next meal. So as a general rule (there are sometimes limited special exceptions to the rule-such as feeding the poor or hungry), Dan would not give anyone a fish. Dan taught all his students how to go out and catch their own fish.

If it took you a year to be able to track an elk all day long through the mountains he would spend the time needed to do the job right. If you did not know the edible plants, he would repeat the lesson again and again until you were comfortable using the plants he taught. He did not expect you to pull out a plant unless you were going to use it in a meal or for medical purposes. He did expect you to be able to identify the plant as he walked and talked with you and know how to use the plant.

So this principal was taught to all his students on many different levels. When he was tracking the elk with Sarah he was teaching her how to track an elk, so if the time ever came that she needed to hunt elk for meat, she would have both the confidence and the skill to track and hunt the elk. Dan taught his student you never hunt for sport, you only hunt for real need. You do not kill an elk when all you need is a single meal. For a single meal a rabbit or a fish will do just fine. When you really need to kill an elk, pray about the matter and if an elk is willing to go into spirit to feed you he will be there for you to kill as you hunt. Sometimes the elk will even show you in your dream where to hunt for him. Never kill any animal for fun.

As they walked in the forest and the high mountain meadows he would also teach her of the edible plants as well as the medical plants they encountered. The tracking of the Spanish Trails was another way Dan was teaching Sarah to fish, by tracking a trail to the buried or hidden caches the Spanish often hid.

As Sarah searched the camp Dan smoked his pipe, and watched his student track or work the metal detector as she searched the camp. Dan might know what was concealed by the camp. Certainly if he asked the Angels around him, they would answer his questions. Yet in the end it was up to Sarah to track the trail. If she caught a fish or recovered a cache it would depend on how much effort and skill she applied in learning her lessons and carrying out the hunt.

In two hours of searching she recovered nothing, Dan suggested she take a break and eat a snack with him. Then Dan suggested to Sarah that maybe she should change her search style from a grid to one where she had an object to hide.

Then he told her to pick twenty hiding places she could come back to and find a small cache that she hid, say next year or ten years from now. So Sarah walked around looking for twenty spots to hide some coins.

Then after she pointed out the twenty sites to Dan she asked, "Well what do you think?"

Dan replied, "It does not matter what I think, you are doing the search and those are the sites you picked; so search them all thoroughly."

An hour later as Sarah walked from the fifth site towards the sixth site the metal detector screamed out loudly. Sarah hollered to Dan, "I found something!"

Getting a small trowel she dug down and there six inches under the soil she found an old fashioned hand forged axe head. If there was a handle, it had long since rotted and returned to the earth. Sarah resumed her search with the metal detector scanning the sites she had selected.

An hour and forty five minutes later, the pulse induction metal detector screamed again. This time Sarah dug down to see what she found before excitedly hollering out to Dan. Again she found a handmade object. This object was worn by horses on their feet (hooves).

"Well," she told Dan, "maybe the horseshoe will bring me luck."

Dan smiled and said, "Well, we have about three more hours until dark. Try and make the most of it."

Three hours later, at the fifteenth site she searched, Sarah got a response on the metal detector.

"I hope it is not another horse shoe or axe head," she said to herself. As she dug down this hole was much deeper about twelve inches, as she hit the object and started to clear the dirt away, she loudly whispered, "Dan come quick, right now!" Dan had put his pipe out and walked up beside Sarah.

Dan told Sarah, "Be careful not to damage what you have found. Take your time and dig all around it."

After Sarah carefully removed the grapefruit-sized chunk of gold ore, she excitedly showed it to Dan. Dan smiled as he was happy that his tracking student had made a wonderful recovery.

Then Dan told Sarah, "Take the metal detector and check the hole to ensure you have recovered everything that was hidden there long ago."

Sarah rescanned the site again and again her metal detector screamed as she approached the hole from the south. Digging down with the garden trowel she again recovered another grapefruit size specimen of pink rose quartz laced with wire gold.

Sarah was overjoyed at her good fortune. Then to show she remembered her lesson that Dan had just taught her Sarah rescanned the hole a third time and again the metal detector screamed as it approached the hole she had dug.

Time after time, as Sarah repeatedly searched the site with the metal detector, each time she uncovered one piece of high-grade gold ore after another. Some of the specimens came from the left or right side of the hole, others were just buried an inch or two deeper than she had dug when she had earlier removed a large chunk of gold in quartz. As she recovered one piece after another, the hole grew wider and deeper. Finally a time came when there was no more response on the metal detector.

There beside her hole were twelve grapefruit-size chunks of pink rose quartz with seams of yellow gold visible everywhere. There were pea-size pieces of gold showing throughout all twelve pieces of high-grade gold ore. These were some of the finest specimens of gold ore that Dan had ever seen. Certainly any collector would consider a single sample of this high grade gold ore the finest specimen in his mineral collection.

Dan then told Sarah it was time to fill in her hole. Then Dan removed from his pack some seeds of red clover and peppermint which were planted in the loose soil in the hole they had refilled. Then Dan told Sarah be sure you give thanks to the spirits living her in love and light which helped you today as well as your Guardian Angel which did a super job of helping you.

Around a camp fire that night they shared a can of chili with some crackers and cheese. They washed the food down with water they had filtered with a water filter, from a stream.

As they sat around the campfire discussing the day's events, they also discussed the selling of the gold specimens and giving 25% to charity. Dan said it is always important to give to charity first as it shows to the universe you are abundantly provided for. If you hoard the recovery and try to keep it all to yourself then you cut off the abundant flow of GOD's universal energy and you block the energy flow so any future recoveries become many times more difficult to occur. Just as refilling your hole is important and replanting plants to help Mother Earth is a nice way to say thank you.

Sarah seemed lost in thought as she watched the fire burning. Then she turned to Dan and said, if it is agreeable with you then let's give 1/3 to charity, four of the chunks of gold. Then there will be four chunks of gold for you and four chunks of gold for me. "Is that ok?" she asked.

Dan was silent as he too was lost in thought. Beside him, his Guardian Angel whispered in his ear, *"I told you so, back at the prayer circle, I told you so, the morning you first met her. I told you she was worth all the tears you would cry and the time you would spend teaching her."*

Then Dan replied to Sarah, "If that is what you chose to do, than that is fine with me."

There had been times in the past when Dan had witnessed similar recoveries of precious metals. Gold often brought out the best and the worst in human nature. Dan had witnessed times when the partners had done their best to kill the other partners as they wanted all the treasure for themselves. There were times when one partner did their best to double cross his fellow partners. Just as there are people who are not very nice, across the fire from him sat a woman who had complete faith in him, she was also willing to go the extra mile and use her money to help those less fortunate and in need.

As the fire burned down low, Sarah seemed lost in thought. Her vacation was about over and she had to get back to her job. Then she thought of James. Now *that* was the kind of man she wanted! He was handsome, smart, he was great in bed. She knew that all she needed was a little money and he would come back to here. She knew she could change him. She would find out what kind of work he liked doing, and she was willing to support him until he found an honest job.

Across the fire from Sarah, two tears ran down Dan's weathered face. For Dan realized Sarah's thoughts and her emotions. Dan would warn Sarah again before she left to Seattle that the man in her thoughts was not a very nice man. Indeed, the old Indian thought, love or infatuation with your dream of a man (or woman) can blind you to the truth.

The following day, Sarah and Dan walked back to Osha Station. There they caught the coal burning steam train back to Antonio, Colorado. Five days later, Sarah was back home in Seattle. Her first call was to James. Her heart beat faster as she talked to him and told her lover she had just struck it rich in Colorado. She excitedly told him how she had just gotten twenty seven thousand dollars from the sale of the treasure she had recovered.

****

It was a stroke of luck, Sarah calling, James thought. It took him about forty seconds of phone conversation to recall the woman. He had classified her in the waste of time file, as soon as he had assessed her financial net worth. He had not had another profitable business venture in nine months since he had gotten back from a memorable and profitable vacation in Acapulco, Mexico with Jackie. It was a good thing he dumped that witch. Why she had called the police and there was an arrest warrant out for him just because he charged a Harley Davison motorcycle on her credit card. Most times, his victims just kept quiet as they were embarrassed by their own stupidity in letting him steal their money.

Sarah was delighted that, after calling James, he still remembered her. So Sarah began telling him the wonderful news of her gold strike in the mountains of Colorado near Osha. She knew James had her on his mind the whole time. Certainly he was in her thoughts. When she told him about her discovery of gold he had promptly invited her out to a fine restaurant for dinner. Well, she smiled to herself, she knew she could get James back.

Sarah was delighted the way the evening had gone. A fine restaurant, fine wine, and an evening of dancing. James could not take his eyes of her. He was even very interested in her prospecting trip. He was very curious about how much gold she had. She explained that the four gold specimens she had had been sold on the internet.

When they got back to her apartment James simply could not control himself. One thing led to another and they ended up on the living room floor as they made love in the heat of passion. Later in the evening they danced to a "Shakira" in the nude.

Sarah showed James the $27,000 in cash she kept hidden in a box beneath the bottom drawer of her dresser. James complemented Sarah on her great luck in making the gold strike. A couple more glasses of wine and they went to sleep in each other's arms. As Sarah drifted off to sleep, her last thought was her wish had come true.

Sarah awoke in the dark. Maybe it was the weight of James getting out of bed that had awaken her, maybe it was the sound of the bottom drawer of her dresser hitting her floor. As she came awake, she saw James removing her cash from her hiding place. James was already dressed and he was grabbing her cash before heading out the door. Sarah jumped out of bed and ran screaming at James to stop.

As she ran up to him, James smashed his fist into Sarah's jaw, instantly breaking it. She reached out with her hands and grabbed one of his legs. James simply used his other leg to kick as hard as he could into Sarah's stomach and ribs. Kick after kick he delivered. Ribs were smashed and broken under his brutal beating. Her right lung collapsed. A kick to her head knocked Sarah unconscious. James walked out of Sarah's life. He had gotten what he wanted, all her money.

****

Twenty-three days later, Sarah was released from the hospital. She walked with a cane and still had difficulty breathing. Going to her job she told the boss what had happened and why she had not been in to work. Her boss informed her that he was sorry but since Sarah had not called in and hand been absent for over three days that was job abandonment he had no choice but to replace her and on Friday he had hired a new secretary. He handed her the last two weeks pay she was owed, eight hundred and forty six dollars. Nine years at a job, and one bad beating which put her into the hospital and now it looked like Sarah was out on the street and might end up homeless. For the next nine days Sarah attempted to arrange two job interviews a day. Fifteen job interviews and not one job. Sarah felt that she might have gotten a job several times with her years of experience except when the interview was conducted her walking cane, slow movements and difficulty breathing resulted in her being passed over.

Returning home to her apartment Sarah saw the second eviction notice posted on her apartment door. That night Sarah felt desperation such as she had not felt in years since her first husband told her he was leaving. That night Sarah prayed to GOD for an hour asking what she was to do. There was no answer, only silence broken by her sobbing and tears of desperation running down her face. Sarah fell asleep crying, she fell asleep laying on her back as that was the only position she could breathe until her ribs healed.

In the morning Sarah packed up her car with all the belongings, dropped her key in the managers mail slot and headed for New Mexico.

****

James was having a really nice day; with the cash in the bank from Jackie and Sarah he felt it was important to keep up his image. Today he was buying a bright red Porsche 911. It dropped his bank account down to two thousand dollars but what the hell, it was worth the ninety two thousand dollars in cash it cost him. He had a hottie (a beautiful woman) he would be picking up later for dinner and some evening delight.

James went and picked up a thousand dollars' worth of cocaine and decided to have a few lines before he tried out his Porsche in the interstate. He wanted to fly. As he left the city and the traffic behind him, James speeded up to seventy five miles per hour (the speed limit was 55 mph on this stretch of the highway). As James relaxed and though about his date tonight he blew a line of cocaine. Looking to his left a car pulled up alongside of him. The driver in the passing lane was looking straight at him. James looked at the old timer who must have been fifty years old. He thought the old man must be crazy wanting to race him. Just look at that old man's haircut, it was so short he could have been in the army, why that style went out in the 1960's.

James thought, "I will show that old man." James speeded his Porsche up to eighty-five miles an hour. The old man in the car beside him speeded up to eighty five miles an hour matching James Porsche speed. That crazy old man James thought, look at that pointed cap the old man wore, it was just like the cap the door man wore at the hotels he stayed at. As James looked again the old man got on his old CB radio. Probably telling his buddies he can beat a Porsche. James smiled as he knew what his Porsche could do. He would play with the old fool a while longer. James speeded up to ninety five miles per hour. The man in the car across from him matched his speed.

When James looked over at the old man again, lying folded on the back of his car seat he had a jacket with a badge on it. Well I will show that key stone cop what this Porsche can do. With that James floored his accelerator and two point five seconds later he hit 188 miles per hour. Looking back in his rear view mirror James saw the car that was beside him flip on his lights and siren. At the next on ramp, two additional California Highway Patrol cars joined the first one.

James smiled, "Well they thought they could just sneak up and arrest him for that Harley Davison motorcycle he had stolen with the credit card, they would have to catch him first."

The police officers had radioed ahead for spike belts to lay across the highway. Up ahead he saw a road block and the police officers were laying down the spike belts as he approached. James swerved into the median to avoid them. His maneuver would have worked except this portion of the grassy median had a pothole made on rainy days by cars turning and running across the median to head the opposite direction on the highway.

James Porsche hit the pot hole at 177 miles per hour and the driver's front tire immediately blew out. Catastrophe followed. Time after time the Porsche rolled until it came to a stop between the two lanes of the highway. It took a team of firemen with "the jaws of life" to cut James out of the wreckage of his Porsche. Paramedics were keeping him alive until he could be rushed to the hospital. A sub dermal hematoma (bleeding of the brain) and a blood clot on the left side of the brain resulted in James having a stroke. The right side of James body no longer worked very well. He had no feeling on his right arm, right leg or the right side of his face. Few could understand what he said when he spoke. James was to receive three months of physical therapy. Without any insurance the hospitals released James and got him back out on the street as quickly as possible.

****4 years later****

Molly and Dancing Wind had just returned from a vacation cruise in Hawaii. They drove up the coast to see Sarah in Seattle. Sarah suggested having dinner on the waterfront by the Seattle Ferry Terminal beside Alaskan Way, but first Sarah took them up to Pikes Market. Here one can see musicians playing banjos, guitars or even pianos for tips, fruit stands were selling dozens of fresh and dried fruits and vegetables, fish markets sell many types of sea food, in store front windows one can see cheese being made.

Dancing Wind was purchasing some dried apples when she noticed a passing woman feeling up the butt of a man whose back was to her. She was surprised to see a woman do this as usually men often engage in this behavior. Then suddenly Dancing Wind realized that the woman who was reaching under the man's coat and feeling his right butt was actually a female pickpocket out practicing her trade. Sarah purchased some goat cheese while Molly purchased a small jar of honey.

Next the teenagers headed down towards the waterfront to find a restaurant to have lunch. Here they went there for a seafood lunch overlooking the water. While eating their seafood they saw the ferry leaving. Eating outside a young boy set down his food down on a wooden table. The boy then got up from his plate of food to throw a piece of trash into the trash can. As the boy moved away from his plate of food a dozen seagulls suddenly flew in besides the boy's plate of food. A dozen seagulls gobbled up the food off the plate.

As the boy ran back to his plate of food waving his arms up and down and yelling at the top of Molly and

Sarah decided to have wild Pacific Salmon from Alaska. Dancing Wind had eaten Albacore Tuna. After paying for their lunch they turned to leave the restaurant.

James had been walking by Fisherman's Wharf when he looked into the window and saw Sarah. It was all her fault he had had the car accident with the new Porsche 911. If she had not lured him to her house with all the cash from her gold mining he would have not purchased the new car so he would not have had the accident. James rushed into the restaurant and rushed Sarah and grabbed her with his left hand by the throat. He was going to pay Sarah back for his years of suffering.

Bystanders at the restaurant yelled to the man attacking the woman, "You better let her go." Yet no one moved in to assist Sarah except Dancing Wind. Molly was about three yards away and she moved in to help Sarah, but she was too far away to be of immediate assistance.

As Sarah was grabbed by the throat, her first reaction was shock as she recognized James. Then her next reaction was anger from the beating he had given her that hospitalized her for a month. This was instantly followed by a front snap kick into James balls. As James started doubling over in pain she stepped in with her left foot and grabbed James hair with both hand jerking his face further down at the same time she violently raised her right knee smashing it into James face. James nose broke under the impact. Blood splattered on James, Sarah and their clothing.

Dancing Winds Guardian Angel yelled to Dancing Wind to "Deflect the fist." Dancing Wind rushed in and grabbed Sarah's right arm as her fist was beginning to form and her right elbow came back. Dancing Winds Guardian Angel had intervened as she realized that Sarah was so mad she was delivering all her force to a location that would have caused irreparable harm to James.

Sarah had started to pivot to her right to deal with the new threat, when she noticed it was her dear friend which stopped her third blow. Dancing Wind then took Sarah's elbow and guided her out of the restaurant and down the block to where their jeep was parked. Dancing Wind placed Sarah in the passenger seat and fastened her seat belt. Molly hopped in the back of the jeep. Then Dancing Wind ran around and jumped into the driver's seat and Dancing Wind started the jeep up and merged the jeep into the traffic.

A few moments later Dancing Wind asked Sarah if she was ok.

Sarah was quiet for a minute and then she asked, "Why did you stop me?"

Dancing Wind replied, "Your Guardian Angel asked mine for help, you were so angry as you executed the counterattack that you were not listening to your Guardian Angel. I only stopped the third blow you were about to deliver."

"Why the third blow?"

"When you calm down you will realize the target you selected, and the force you were using. I did not want you to kill him," Dancing Wind replied.

Sarah said under her breath, "You do not know what he did to me. He almost beat me to death. I spent a month in the hospital and four months recovering from the beating he gave me. He would have killed me if the doctors in the hospital had not been able to save my life. So, as Dan says, Let him have the Karma.

"It's GOD's place to judge not yours. No one has the right to judge another. Besides, look at it this way, Are you better off now or four years ago when you were dating James? That S.O.B. was the catalyst that got you to spending more time with Dan and developing your spiritual side of your character. Now, when you are not fighting mad, you usually talk to and listen to the advice of your Guardian Angels. Would you really like to go back to working and dating men like James?"

Sarah replied, "I would not touch a snake like that even with a ten-foot pole."

Dancing Wind replied, "I will bet, six or seven years ago, you would have dropped everything for a date with him. Apparently he still has the same hot temper as when he lunged for your throat. I do not think you would have lived 'happily ever after' with James. It would have been a trip to the hospital every month, until he killed you from his beatings. He never would have stayed with you. He is really just an alligator destroying numerous women's lives."

Turning the conversation to a lighter note, Dancing Wind added, "If you had not come back to New Mexico, you would not have gotten to meet me. Then where would you be? Who else takes you to the vacation hot spots like Canada del Oro where you can be in foot races where, if you lose the race, you lose your life. That day you lost your two-thousand-dollar backpack, didn't that Spanish death trap get your adrenaline pumping? Am I a good friend or what? Who else takes you out to lunch so you can demonstrate your Tae Kwon Do (Korean karate)?"

As they drove along the coastline, Sarah turned to Dancing Wind and Molly, and asked, "What really brings you two up to Seattle? You do not strike me as two ladies who drive 1,400 miles just to take a friend out to a seafood dinner."

"Well, we came up to invite you on a treasure-hunting trip to southern New Mexico. It seems that, in the 1880s, a man from Odessa, Texas named Ben Sublet said he discovered gold in the Guadalupe Mountains which are located west of Carlsbad, New Mexico. Many times over a period of years, Ben Sublet returned to Odessa with his gold. It seems he must of cached gold at different locations as sometimes when followed he just went into the Guadalupe Mountains on the southern end and then returned to Odessa with his gold nuggets. One time he took his son Ross to his mine and the boy said his father lowered himself down into a crevice on a rope. The boy remained on the top of the ground while his father lowered himself down

198 • Barton R Thom

into the crevice where he gathered up the gold nuggets."

Sarah was silent a few moments while she framed her reply. "I am always interested in going prospecting and treasure hunting with you, but I have some serious concerns about looking for gold in the Guadalupe Mountains. Isn't Carlsbad where the underground nuclear wastes are stored?

"Yes," Molly replied, "but we will not go anywhere near the waste site."

Sarah replied, "As I recall reading somewhere, the nuclear wastes are stored in salt beds hundreds of feet thick. Certainly an area of salt deposits formed by the ocean (salt water) is not a favorable location for a rich placer gold deposit. Neither is the area around Carlsbad Caverns which is at the southern end of the Guadalupe Mountains favorable for gold as I recall the cave formation and the adjoining area is lime stone. If the lime stone was formed by deposit of hundreds of feet of marine crustaceans, certainly it too would have little chance of having a rich mineral deposit."

"I too have read about Ben Sublets gold and while the basic facts are true, I just do not want to get involved in a wild goose chase. When I did some early research into the matter it simply was a no go as a project without a major break or some new leads." Then Dancing Wind turned to Molly and said, "Hand Sarah the file from the brief case."

The file had come out of the New Mexico Records center and Spanish Archives. The file was from the

Federal Writers Project of the 1930's and was titled "The Lost Burro Mine." The story detailed how, in the 1800s, a man, Juan Tores, lived south of Albuquerque was known to have lots of gold and ever fall he would throw a big party. While everyone was having fun at the party he would mount up on his large burro and ride to the south east towards the Guadalupe Mountains. There he would get his gold and then return a week or two later with lots of gold. Finally the day came when he threw a large party and rode out never to return again.

Years passed and sometimes people spoke of Juan Tores and wondered what had happened to him as well as where he got his gold. Well the old Hispanic telling the story said he had gone over to the Guadalupe Mountains to hunt elk for meat, for while there are no elk in the Guadalupe Mountains now back a hundred years ago there were.

The Hispanic man told the writer how while over at the Broke Off Mountains immediately west of the Guadalupe Mountains he had gone do a deep crevice on the North end of the Broke Off Mountains and here on the north end is a deep crevice or rift where there is water in the bottom. They had gone there for water. Nearby he found a large dead burro with a man beside the burro. The man had his skull blown apart by a bullet. On the saddle horn of the dead burro the man found 110 ounces of placer gold. At today's prices for gold that gold would be worth $110,000!

Sarah was lost in thought. The account from the Spanish Archives changed everything. In her mind, it all began to make sense. Ben Sublet had lied about where he got the gold. He had told everyone—all his new found friends and drinking buddies—that his gold came from the Guadalupe Mountains, to throw them off the trail of where the gold really came from. The Broke Off Mountains were adjacent to the Guadalupe Mountains and their entire geological structure was different.

Yes this just might work Sarah thought, she had ten days of vacation coming from Wal-Mart. If they went on Friday she could get sixteen days off because of the weekends. Sarah asked for the time off work and was given it starting next weekend. Sarah and Molly spent the week waiting for Sarah exploring the San Juan Islands in a Cape Dory they rented from a marina in Seattle, Washington.

When the jeep was packed, Dancing Wind, Molly O'Brian, and Sarah took off down Interstate 5 to Sacramento. The reason they did not take the direct route on Interstate 90 to Interstate 82 then to 84 is they did not want to get caught by a winter storm in the mountains. From Sacramento they continued south to Bakersfield (there are lots of oil wells here) and San Bernardino. Where they picked up Interstate 10 headed for El Paso, Texas.

As they approached El Paso they got a phone call from Dan that diverted them from heading to Carlsbad and instead, they headed for Sierra Blanco, Texas.

Dan's logic was, he recalled seeing a Spanish Trail crossing the Interstate 10 at mile marker #98 (Latitude 31 degrees 12 minutes and 49.3 sec, Longitude 105 degrees, 29 minutes and 38.2 seconds) headed north towards the Guadalupe Mountains. Years earlier he had driven across Texas and recalled seeing a Spanish monumented trail coming up from the south and dozens of Spanish Markers were located by a rest stop on the south side of the highway on the north end of a ridge of mountains. The highway passed to the north end of these Spanish Markers, which were easily accessible due to the rest stop. The Spanish Markers had been heavily marked up with graffiti but they would not prevent the women from reading the markers and learning the messages they held.

Sarah asked Dan as they talked at the rest stop, "Why, if you feel the trail is leading up to the Guadalupe Mountains, don't we just start at the Guadalupe Mountains instead of fifty five miles south of them?"

Dan told Sarah, "There are times, when tracking a trail, when it is necessary to jump track a trail, skipping ahead to where you think the trail is going. If a child is lost out in the desert without water certainly jump tracking may work if you can get into the child's mind and see how he/she is thinking. Adults are usually more predictable and even easier to jump track.

"In this case, you are tracking a trail made centuries ago, and you are fortunate to have still existing stone monuments marking the trail. I want you to track the trail from well south of the Guadalupe Mountains for four reasons.

"First, you need more experience tracking. Second you will be learning the style of the monument makers and how they thought. So this will help you when the trail gets difficult to track. Third is, you have the opportunity to discover any Spanish Stone Maps which may be along the trail which may give you exact directions to your objective. And finally, it may just be that the location that Ben Sublet got his gold, and that Juan Tories got his gold and the Spanish got their gold just may all be the same place.

"So, if you are tracking this trail and it leads you to your objective then isn't that a lot better than trying to search hundreds of square miles of mountains?"

Sarah and Molly replied, "Well, now that we understand your reasoning, it makes sense to us."

So Dan told the two teenagers to take off in the lead and find the trail he'd spoken of. "You cannot always be following me, for your best learning experiences will occur when you lead and I just follow along."

So Dancing Wind got in Dan's old Ford diesel pickup and rode with him, and they talked about tracking. Molly and Sarah rode in the Jeep, and they were in the lead as they drove East across Texas looking for the Spanish Trail and the rest stop where it crossed the highway.

When they located the rest stop with the Spanish Monuments they parked their vehicles and looked them over doing their best to learn all they could. Then Dan told Molly and Sarah to take their packs along with two gallons of water each and follow the trail North.

"If you need us, get your CB transmitter and antenna to the highest mountain around and give us a call."

Molly gave Dancing Wind her jeep keys and the two women crossed the interstate headed north. Dan and Dancing Wind would take the two vehicles and follow along as best they could.

As Molly and Sarah hiked north in the desert, Dan and Dancing Wind watched them become smaller and smaller the further they traveled until they simply disappeared from sight. Then Dan turned to Dancing Wind and said, "Well kid, are you hungry? Let's go get something to eat."

As Sarah and Molly walked north in the Sonoran Desert, they followed the Old Spanish Trail. Often what originally had been flat ground was now a dry wash as, over the centuries, erosion had cut the trail deeper and deeper.

After an hour Sarah turned to Molly and said, "Here we are, getting all the fun and the experience, and I will bet you they are like two mother hens, worried sick about us and waiting for us to call on our radios."

Back at Sierra Blanco, the two trackers were enjoying a long leisurely hot lunch. Dancing Wind was asking Dan about his hunch on the Spanish Mining gold in the Guadalupe Mountains, and Dan replied, "Well I had seen this trail years ago so it was always there in the back of my mind. But one thing or another always came up so I never had a chance to track this trail."

"With you talking about Ben Sublet's gold in the Guadalupe Mountains., then your talk about the document you found in the NM records center and Spanish Archives. In addition I recall reading about some outlaws robbing the stage coaches running between El Paso and Dallas, Texas. Rumor had it they stayed in a cave near a stone face on the south end of the Guadalupe Mountains. Now, what if the trail Sarah and Molly are following leads right up to the stone face and it is actually a Spanish Marker on a trail leading to the old Spanish Mines? So what do you want to bet that all the little bits of data are really connected?"

Dancing Wind replied, "I don't want to bet against you. I would just be throwing my money away. Besides, my Guardian Angel already told me as you were talking to me that the stone face on the south end of the Guadalupe Mountains is a Spanish Marker."

"So, young lady, are you holding two conversations at once?" Dan asked with a grin on his face.

Dancing Wind smiled at Dan and mischievously replied, "Only when I am verifying the accuracy of what I am being told."

Dan smiled at his student and said to her, "You're coming along fine."

"So, if you are showing off, are Molly and Sarah doing ok? And how many miles have they covered, while you are kicked back and lazing around?"

"Give me a minute," Dancing Wind replied. After putting a White Light of Protection around herself, Dancing Wind asked her Guardian Angel how her friends were doing and how many miles they had covered. Then she thanked her Guardian Angel for the help and the information. Dancing Wind turned to Dan and said, "Our partners have covered seven miles and they are doing fine."

Dan then asked Dancing Wind, "Is there a storm coming in from the west off the California coast?"

Dancing Wind paused to talk with her Guardian Angel, then she replied to Dan's question. "The question was poorly worded, unless you are just checking if you can throw me. Yes, there are always storms and weather fronts moving from the Pacific Ocean towards the Atlantic sea coast. But to clarify your question, in my mind I just asked if there would be a major storm along our tracking path any time in the next five days and the answer was, no." Again Dancing Wind thanked her Guardian Angel for her assistance.

Dan asked Dancing Wind if she realized why he asked her a series of questions. He knew she did not have the answer.

Dancing Wind replied, "The real reason you are asking me a long series of questions is you are teaching me to think about possible difficulties that

can occur when tracking a trail, and you want me to
interact with my Guardian Angel. You want us to be
like two good friends interacting with each other. For
certainly my Guardian Angel is my very best friend."

When you can be distracted, tired, or preoccupied
you want to have that relationship with your Guardian
Angel so that your Angel can instantly interrupt you or
get your attention, and you instantly drop everything
and pay attention to your Guardian Angel. That is why
Dan had insisted that all his students with whom he
taught tracking could instantly be interrupted by their
Guardian Angel and be told: "Danger is approaching."
"You are Clear of Danger." "You are going in the right
direction." And "You are going in the wrong direction."

Dan told Dancing Wind that this trip is really for
Sarah, every day I want you to work with her and her
Guardian Angel so that she can recognizes danger. No
woman should ever be hurt or hospitalized by a
dangerous person. I want you to help Sarah so she can
recognize a dangerous person or situation.

These were the most basic of interactions that one
can have with one's Guardian Angel, that can warn you
of danger and how to move away from the source of
the danger. It is not your Guardian Angel's job to
literally protect your life ... IT IS YOUR
RESPONSIBILITY TO PROTECT YOUR PHYSICAL LIFE ...
IT IS YOUR ANGEL'S RESPONSIBILITY TO WARN YOU
OF DANGER AND TO SHOW YOU THE PROPER
SPIRITUAL DECISIONS ... IT IS UP TO YOU DO MAKE
THE CORRECT DECISIONS ... TO TAKE THE ACTIONS

NEEDED TO SAVE YOUR LIFE ... FOR GOD HAS GIVEN YOU FREE CHOICE.

To the extent you listen to your Guardian Angel, your Guardian Angel will always match you in effort, if you are really trying to do things right. The more effort you make in interacting with the Angels, the more effort the Angels will make in interacting with you!

If you do not listen to the Angel's advice or counsel, the Guardian Angel that watches over you will simply stand back and watch. They appreciate it when you sincerely come to them for advice, and they will go out of their way to help you. On the other hand, if talking to you is like talking to a stone wall ... if you do not listen or you always blow off their advice ... they will stand back and let you learn the hard way. And I can assure you, you do not want to learn the hard way.

Now, if you are open to the concept, you will find that many in the spirit realm will go out of their way to help you if you, in turn, will listen to or interact with them. The Rain Spirits, the Snow Pixies, the Clouds Spirits, the Wind Spirits, the Lightning Spirits, the Water Spirits, Plant Spirits, spirits of every nature, all may interact with you, if take the time to work with and interact with them.

The first step is to interact with the Guardian Angels in a positive and loving manner. Then try and develop relationships with other spirits whom are of love, light peace and unity.

Later that afternoon Dan dropped Dancing Wind off with Sarah and Molly. Then each evening Dan seemed to appear or know where they would be camping and he set up a overnight camp for their arrival.

****

For four days the teenagers traveled north by northeast traveling towards the Guadulope Mountains.

On the first day they passed and left behind Sierra Blanca or the White Shining Mountain as early explores referred to it. Early the second morning they crossed the north south highway 1111. This was the last paved road they would see in the next two days. Often as they hiked towards the north they encountered dirt road running towards the numerous oil and gas wells. The further they proceeded towards the north the more frequent their encounters with trucks doing maintenance or hauling oil or gas. Every night they met with Dan and who had set up a camp for them. Dan also supplied them with fresh water every night for in this harsh dry land water was essential for life. On the fourth day Dancing Wind, Molly and Sarah reached the southern most portion of the Guadalupe Mountains.

It was here Lily, Dancing Winds Guardian Angel led the way towards the western side of the mountain and as they traveled through the Guadalupe Mountain National Park they were joined by Dan who trailed behind the teenagers. When the teenagers stopped to let him join them he made it clear we was simply watching them and observing how they tracked. Then he let them take off tracking the trail while he deliberately trailed behind them and watched.

On the southern end of the mountains they observed a huge face as well as a cave yet they continued following the trail north. Several hours later suddenly a skirimish line of Apache spirits appeared in front of the trackers. Some of the Apaches had old single shot rifles, others held bow and arrows. All the Apaches clearly blocked their path forward.

Immediately Dancing Wind, Molly and Sarah reinforced their White Light of Protection. Dancing Wind, Molly and then Sarah immediately began receiving their danger approaching signals from their Guardian Angels. The teenagers stopped dead in their tracks. Dancing Wind slowly moved forward to talk with one of the Apache spirits. He told Dancing Wind she was not welcome here yet.

The Apache told Dancing Wind, "You and your friends can go no further. You are not welcome here now."

Dancing Wind asked,"When will be allowed to track this trail?"

The Apache replied, "You will be welcome to track this trail as well as to come and drum and dance with us when you can hear without using your ears, when you can see without using your eyes and when you chose to drum with us because it is with that is what you chose in your heart to do."

210 of Barton R Thom

Dancing Wind was silent and lost in thought for a few minutes. In her head she was working out when such events would come to pass in the future.

Dancing Wind realized or maybe the Apache put the thought in her head that it would be many years out in the future before she could possibly hear with out using her ears and see without using her eyes and it probably would not occur in this life time.

Dancing Wind was not willing to use force to cross the line of Apaches so the trail ended here for the teenagers.

As Dan drove the teenagers towards Carlsbad so they could all eat dinner after a very long day Sarah turned toward Dan and asked, "Was this lesson for me?"

Dan smiled and replied, "You hit the nail on the head with the hammer. I wanted you all to encounter danger in a controlled manner so you would clearly feel when your Guardian Angels were warning you of danger.

By having your effort and energy focused on tracking a trail I wanted you all to realize when your Guardian Angel is warning you of danger as well as realize not every trail can be safely tracked all the way.

Some trails, just like some people you have to walk away from."

Beauty is in the Water
Beauty is in the Snow
Beauty is in Love
Just beginning to Grow

A Matter of Integrity

The USS Sophie was certainly one of America's finest cruise ships. There was only one place the USS Sophie cruised with her cruise ship passengers, and that was the vacation hot spot of the beautiful Hawaiian Islands.

If one wanted a relaxing vacation cruise you certainly could not go wrong taking a five day cruise in American's vacation paradise. Deep blue oceans, blue skies, warm tropical weather, and excellent food awaited the two teenagers. So Molly and Dancing Wind hopped a jet plane out of San Francisco for the Hawaiian Islands.

Jim, Molly and Dancing Wind had just spent two months prospecting out in America's unknown vacation paradise, the Gila Mountains, the Tinajas Altas Mountains and the Lechuguilla Desert. They had enjoyed the hot baking sun, no running water, brutal work, hundred degree temperatures and relaxing burro ride across the length of the Lechuguilla Desert from which their sore bottoms were still recovering.

They had left Jim in San Francisco alone so that he had time to think and choose the path he wished to embark upon in his life, now that he had the financial resources and determination to choose a new path in life. So, to make it up to her dearest friend and partner Molly O'Brian, Dancing Wind had suggested a vacation cruise aboard the luxury cruise liner the USS Sophie in the exotic Hawaiian Islands.

Molly was excited about a wonderful vacation, but knowing Dancing Wind she had her doubts and thought that Dancing Wind was up to something. Molly's last vacation to San Francisco, had gotten side tracked with a two month prospecting trip into the hot desert sands south of Yuma, and so she was suspicious of Dancing Winds wonderful offer.

As she looked Dancing Wind over carefully her eyes focused on the Dancing Winds face, her brown eyes and long black hair braided into two pony tails, carefully studying her for any hint it was a joke or that the Indian girl might have a trick up her sleeve.

Dancing Wind shrugged her shoulders, holding her arms out with the palms up. "It's just a vacation for us," she told her dear friend Molly. As an afterthought she added, "My Guardian Angel Lily suggested the trip."

The USS Sophie was the pride of the American Merchant Marine. She was a thousand feet long and she was a painted pristine white. Now days there were few passenger ships left in the United States Merchant Marine. The USS Sophie was the largest passenger ship in operation measuring a thousand feet long. The ship cruised among the Hawaiian Islands making two stops at Hawaii and a stop at Maui on a typical five day cruise.

On the second night of the cruise, Dancing Wind awoke at three in the morning and took a walk towards the stern (back) of the ship. As she approached the stern she saw an old ship's steward, holding fast to the guard railing.

Dancing Wind walked up beside the old man who had picked this quiet time when everyone is normally asleep to quietly drop off the stern of the ship, as his method of suicide. Howard thought dropping off the stern into the ocean would be a quiet peaceful way to end his life. As he started to climb over the rail, his thoughts of death were disturbed by the voice of a teenage girl beside him.

"It is not a painless way to die. The propellers will churn you around, sending you spinning through the water in a giant circle. After you hit the water, you will be crying out to GOD - - 'What have I done!' Then you will be kicking and paddling with your arms, trying to get to the surface as your lungs scream for air. On the way down, the propeller wash will rupture your ear drums and intense pain will sweep through your body. As you complete one revolution, the churning water will not allow you to get a breath before taking you down deep again. Between the second and third complete loop, as you are carried down deep in a circle and you can no longer hold your breath, you will die."

"You want to know what is really ironic when you climb over the rail tonight?" Dancing Wind asked to see if the old steward would talk.

The ship's steward remained quiet as he listened to the teenage girl as she spoke to him. How did she know he was getting up the nerve to climb over the railing and drop into the Pacific Ocean below him? he wondered.

"When you were in heaven and chose your life mission, it was to simply be a man of integrity and not hurt anyone. Literally, your life's purpose was to be a simple man of integrity.

"You see, in your previous life, you worked for a meat packing house in Chicago in the 1800s. You had a family and just barely got by on your wages of two dollars a day supporting your wife and family. You butchered beef and cut it up into the different cuts of meat. They brought you an old dead steer which had died in the train box cars and told you to butcher it. You went and told the boss, 'the steer's meat was already rotten (the meat had already spoiled).'

"The boss told you, 'I want you to butcher it any way and mix the bad meat in with the good meat so no one would notice.'

"When you told the boss, 'Somebody can die of food poisoning.'

"He shrugged his shoulders and said, 'Well, that is their tough luck. Now you make your own luck. You either butcher the steer like I told you, or you're fired, and you will be "Black Balled," so there won't be any work for you anywhere in Chicago.'

"You butchered the steer like you were told. You later learned that five people died from the rotten meat they purchased. A year later, your son died when your wife purchased some rotten meat on sale at the butcher's shop. For literally, what comes around, goes around. That's what karma means. And your karma came back and hit you hard. I know that you would have given your life to save your favorite son's life, but there was nothing you could do. Your son died of food poisoning."

"You swore on your son's grave you would be a man of integrity and not serve anyone bad meat ever again. When you got to heaven—and you did get to heaven--you selected your lessons for this life. The main lesson you chose to experience or practice in this life time was: *YOU CHOSE TO BE A SIMPLE MAN OF INTEGRITY AND NOT HURT ANYONE!*

"It sounds simple but it was a difficult lesson wasn't it? What was it now—let's see—wasn't it about ten years ago when you worked on that heavy lift cargo ship when they loaded your ship up with almost half a ton of spoiled meat?"

"How do you know about that," he asked?

"Well, to tell you the truth, the reason I am talking kind of slow is, your Guardian Angel is telling me the story right now. He is desperately trying to keep you from committing suicide and making the biggest mistake in your life."

216 • Barton R Thom

"He is telling me about your life's purpose and how you handled the hardest test of your life. He told me how there was box after box of meat being loaded on the ship and how it filled up the passage way until you and your men had a chance to load it in the freezer. It was the cook, wasn't it, who pulled out six steaks to cook up for the teenagers? The shore-side port steward had arranged to have six out-of-work teenagers help you load about five tons of supplies. As the cook pulled out the steaks, he was the one who first noticed something wrong with all the steaks. Wasn't it over six pounds of T-bone steaks, that were all spoiled? Then he rubbed his bare hand across one of the raw steaks and rubbed his two palms together, rapidly back and forth. Everyone started to back away from the cook's hands as the smell of rotten meat filled the galley (ships kitchen)."

The old steward recalled the event like it was yesterday. Suddenly he began telling the story. Dancing Wind smiled to herself and to Lily, the Guardian Angel standing beside her.

"Yeah, I guess I remember it like it was yesterday. I was on a heavy lift ship in San Diego, headed through the Panama Canal to Baton Rouge, Louisiana.

"It was in the last two hours, just before we sailed and put to sea. The supplies had been ordered four days earlier. I thought we would sail before the food provisions I ordered would arrive. The port steward told the teenagers loading the supplies that they would each get a steak dinner. I told Mac, my cook to pull out six steaks and cook them however the teenagers wanted them done.

"We were still unloading the supplies off the truck, when Mac came up and told me the meats were all spoiled. The truck driver had just handed me the invoices to sign, as he was in a hurry to leave. I could see it in his face and eyes, he knew. I just knew that he knew, that he had delivered a spoiled load of meat. I threw the invoices back into his face and I told him I was not signing anything until we inspected every case of meat!"

****3 Days earlier****

Samuel was having a bad day. The refrigeration unit was broken down on the refrigerated cargo box he hauled meat in. The boss had told him it didn't matter, as he was just hauling it down to San Diego and it was only a ten hour drive. The meat will keep without refrigeration for ten hours he was told. That had been three days ago when he picked up the load of meat and the United States government certification/Dept. of Agriculture, that the cargo of meat was all grade "A" inspected beef.

The boss of the Mexicali Meat Company of Juarez was Jackson. He was always trying to save a buck by not performing any maintenance on their company vehicles. So the boss, Jackson, had told Samuel to pick up the load of meats, even though the refrigeration was not working. Maybe the meats could have been delivered in one day. Yet, as Samuel's truck broke down again, on the side of the road, he knew the cargo would spoil.

The first break down was a simple flat tire, only there was a five-hour delay getting a spare tire brought to him, as there was no spare tire on the truck. The second breakdown that day was caused by the engine overheating. Without a new water pump the truck was not going anywhere.

Samuel told his boss, "I am going to need a refrigerated truck to transfer the meat too before it spoils."

Samuel's boss, Jackson, told him to just wait and another truck would be coming. They just had to deliver their cargo first.

Samuel waited by his truck all day. And the next day Samuel was still there on the side of the road waiting. The temperature in the refrigerated reefer (the freezer cargo box where the meat was supposed to be kept frozen) had climbed to ninety degrees.

That evening another refrigerated truck arrived. The meat was beginning to smell pretty bad. Samuel's boss told the drivers, "Just freeze the meat in the second truck and get it to the ship. If it is frozen, they will not notice the meat is spoiled until it is out to sea. Then we can always blame it on the ship. After all, they have a US Dept. of Agriculture certificate showing the meat is all grade 'A.' When the cargo gets loaded and the invoices are signed, it will be too late. Mexicali Meat

Company of Juarez will have already gotten their money."

****

Samuel called his boss Jackson and told him, "They are refusing to sign the invoices, Boss. It looks bad. Now they are examining every case of meat."

Jackson said, "Just keep pressing them to sign the invoices and do not leave. I will send Robert over to help you get the invoices signed."

The boss turned to Robert and said, "Get on a clean white lab coat and go reassure them the meats are government inspected. Show them the certification and get those invoices signed. I do not want any excuses."

****

"So, what did you do next?" Dancing Wind asked the old ship steward.

"I did my best to cover my ass," he replied.

"First, I called the shipping company attorney—I think his name was Rawlings—and advised him of the situation. I told him the meat was rotten and it would likely kill anyone who ate it."

He told me, "...by all means get rid of the meat immediately. We just had seventeen men hospitalized from food poisoning on another heavy lift ship. It had to alter course and put into a port in Mexico as so many men had to be hospitalized. It was the same meat supplier. Just do not sign the invoices. Don't worry, just follow my advice and I will take care of everything."

****

"What did you do after talking to the attorney?"

"I followed his advice and refused to sign anything. Then, I called the union hall and told them they had just delivered a load of spoiled meat to the ship. I insisted on talking to the head man there, Hood.

"He told me, '....by all means do not serve the meat. Just get rid of it. I would go there right now, but I am just too busy here at the union hall. Just let me know what happens, and I will support you 100%.'"

****

"So you covered all the bases, didn't you? It sure sounded like you tried to do it right."

"Well, I also called the Mexicali Meat Company and told them they delivered a bad load of beef which had already spoiled. I told them they needed to pick up this load of beef and deliver another. All they did was give me the run around about picking up the spoiled beef. They told me they were sending a meat inspector, and that I was mistaken; as it was all grade 'A' beef."

****

"Next, a man drives up to the ship in a car. This guy steps out in a white lab coat and says he is here to inspect the meats to assure me they are quality meats. As we are standing there I notice he is not driving a US government vehicle so I have my doubts he is a real Department of Agriculture, government meat inspector. So I ask to see his official government ID. Well I do not have a government ID he tells me. I am an employee of the slaughter house."

****

"So the man accompanied me aboard the ship. There he talks to Samuel the driver of the meat truck and he gets the invoices and the certificate from him.

"Then this inspector tells me, 'The meats are all government-inspected grade "A" beef.' Then he walks down the corridor or passageway, past the meat. You can already smell the meat is spoiled. Without opening a single box he says, 'Yes, it is all here, like on the invoices. This is the grade "A" beef of the Mexicali Meat Company sent over. Just sign here.'

"So then, I reached into a box of meat and removed a cut of meat. I ran both of my bare hands over the cut of meat. Then I rubbed my hands rapidly together; the stench of the spoiled meat was overpowering. As I walked towards the inspector, he kept backing up as he rapidly back-peddled in his haste to get away from me. I told him to take his rotten meat and get it off this ship."

"What happed next?" Dancing Wind asked.

"Samuel and the meat inspector refused to take any of the meats. They got in their vehicles and drove off."

****

"Then a US Customs inspector who had been watching the entire series of events walked up to the cases of meat. He pulled out a notebook, and jotted down the box numbers and weights of each case of meat as he individually examined each one. Then he went up to the ship captains office and asked for the official ships log book. For ten minutes the US Customs officer wrote in the ships log book. Then he told the ship's captain he needed four copies, which the captain made for the US customs officer. As the US Customs officer went to leave the ship he handed two copies to me.

"Then I asked the customs officer if he had two minutes. I wanted to mail a letter.

"The officer said, 'It's no trouble at all, I'll be happy to mail a letter for you.'

"Then I quickly wrote a letter and handed it to the US Customs officer. Then I told him, 'Thank you.'

"Then, as he turned to leave the ship he said, 'Have a good day.'

"I mailed a copy of the paper the US Customs Officer had given me to my attorney. Thirty minutes later, the ship sailed for the Panama Canal on the way to Louisiana."

****

Two days later, when the ship was a hundred miles off shore, the fourteen cases of bad meat were dumped over the side of the ship and into the Pacific Ocean. For even today, the US military warships, cargo ships, passenger ships and tankers simply throw their trash over the side of the ship polluting the ocean.

People still have a long way to grow up, before they cease polluting our Mother Earth. As a society and a people we have to realize we cannot keep dumping our trash everywhere. We need to dispose of our trash properly before we turn the entire surface of the earth into our own personal trash dump. When you walk upon the sandy beaches of any shore line, anywhere in the world, you will find the trash washed up on the sandy beaches from passing ships.

Unless the practice is outlawed, just like dumping oil in the oceans, it will continue. For that is what lazy, and irresponsible people do, they leave a trail of trash where ever they go.

****

The heavy-lift ship arrived in Baton Rouge, Louisiana two weeks later. Howard was in his office working on placing a new order for provisions for the

ship. The knock on his office door told him he had
visitors. Opening the door, he saw three angry men.
Jackson of Mexicali Meat Company was there, along
with his attorney. A union man was there beside them,
and they were ready to read Howard the riot act.

Jackson told the steward, "I am here to collect
$20,000 for the meats you dumped over the side of the
ship, and the damages you have done to the reputation
of Mexicali Meat Company. If you pay me now, I will
not take all your vehicles, your house and life savings,
too, when I sue you in court for libel (hurting a
person's reputation by telling lies in writing) and
slander (hurting a person's reputation by verbally
saying lies) for ruining my companies reputation."

Jackson's attorney Fergerson said, "Let's review the
facts of this case, and we will give you chance to settle
this matter for just $20,000.00 otherwise we will be
completely justified to also sue you for an additional $
20,000.00 in punitive damages (courts award punitive
damages to punish an individual for their actions) as
you have committed both slander as well as your libel
against our excellent reputation which the Mexicali
Meat Company of Juarez works tirelessly to maintain.

"This is what we will be presenting in court if you
are foolish enough to fight us." Fergerson opened his
brief case and pulled out the first document. "First ,we
have a sworn statement from the union official at San
Diego.

"It reads, and I quote, 'I have never spoken to
anyone aboard the heavy-lift ship about any problems

with meat deliveries from Mexicali Meat Companies. Had I known of any problems with the quality of food being delivered to any ship we represent, I would have immediately dropped everything and investigated the matter. I have never spoken with the ships steward Howard. In fact I simply have never heard of him before you asked.'

"Our second piece of evidence will be a statement from the US government meat inspector saying that he personally inspected the truck load of meat and it was all grade 'A' beef.

"The third piece of evidence will be the notarized statement by the truck driver, Samuel.

"He says that, as soon as you saw the boxes of T-bone and rib-eye steaks my company delivered to your ship, you went berserk, and threw the invoices he politely asked you to sigh in his face. It also says here that you threatened his life if he did not remove the cases of T-Bone and Rib-Eye Steaks from the ship.

"Even worse, he quotes you as saying, 'You would not feed the men on your ship anything but dog food as the seaman you worked with, were as low as dogs, and dog food was good enough for them! Clearly the ships steward has emotional or mental difficulties.'

"The fourth piece of evidence will be the Statement of our Quality Control inspector for the Mexicali Meat Company, and how he tried to show you the US government inspection certificate and you refused to look at it. Then he personally inspected the fourteen cases of T-bone Steaks and Rib-eye Steaks and how you said, "... you would rather throw them over the side of the ship than feed them to the low life scum (crew), I work with on this ship."

"The fifth piece of evidence is the affidavit by the shipping company attorney Rawlings.

"Now, you have been slandering us, saying Rawlings told you to get rid of the meat. Certainly if you wish to see Rawlings' affidavit it contradicts you completely. Let's see, and I am quoting it exactly word for word, '...Mexicali Meat Company has always provided high quality meats to our shipping company for ten years. We have never had any problems what so ever. As for Mr. Howard's claim, I spoke with him and told him, '...by all means get rid of it the meat immediately. We just had seventeen men hospitalized from food poisoning on another heavy-lift ship. It had to alter course and put into a port in Mexico as so many men had to be hospitalized. It was the same meat supplier. Just do not sign the invoices. Don't worry, just follow my advice and I will take care of everything." The statement is completely false; I never spoke with the man. I do not even know what he is talking about, certainly I would remember a serious matter such as he is speaking of, and investigate it thoroughly."

Mike, the union representative then told Howard, "We cannot have mentally unstable individuals working aboard out ships. You are going to have to pay for the steaks you destroyed by throwing over the side of the ship. I am going to have to ask you to get off the ship now. Howard, you are going to be lucky, very lucky, if anyone ever allows you to work on their ship ever again!"

Fergerson reached into his open brief case. "Now, here is a written apology to Jackson and the Mexicali Meat Co. for your defamation of their fine character. It simply explains how you lied about everything. The second pages is a promissory note with a payment schedule where you are going to pay the Mexicali Meat company $1,000 dollars a month for the next twenty-four months to pay for the meats you threw over the side of the ship, plus interest of course. You are lucky we are giving you a chance to apologize and pay restitution.

"Of course, if you don't sign these papers now, our generous offer to you is off the table. We will sue you for everything you have! We will take your house, your car your savings, stocks, bank accounts; you will have nothing left when we finish with you! We will find all your assets and take everything you have! You won't have a job or a penny to your name if we have to go to court to get justice!"

"I sent for the cook and the butcher, who had examined the meats when the ship was docked at San Diego. Both men told the men present that the meats were already spoiled when delivered to the ships."

Fegerson (Mexicali Meat Company's attorney) replied, "I will get their testimony thrown out of court, as you are their boss, they are just saying that as they are dependent upon you for their job. Those men's testimony simply will not hold up in court. I will have their testimony excluded before the trial even starts. You're on your own here, Howard."

"That meat was rotten and you damn well know it," Howard replied.

Fegerson smiled and replied, "We will never know, will we? It is on the bottom of the Pacific Ocean now. Somebody is going to pay for that meat, and it looks like you will. Now sign the papers, or you will find I have the political pull here to have you served with a law suit within an hour.

"Face it Howard, nobody will stand beside you. You're all alone, you have no evidence and you certainly will not beat the stacked deck I have here."

Howard, leaned back on his chair and smiled as he replied, "Why don't you sewer rats go back into the hole you crawled out of. There is just one problem, you crooks seem to have overlooked. Some people have integrity. And that is why you are not going to sue me. You see, there will be lots of publicity over a public trial, and since you will lose in the end, your attorney Fegerson will not allow you to make such a stupid decision when he knows you will lose both from the publicity as well as the legal judgment."

Howard turned to the attorney and said, "Why don't you tell Jackson and his Mexicali Meat Company why they are going to drop this case today and get out of my office."

"As I am sure you know, Fegerson, (and the attorney had no idea what it was Howard was speaking of) the US government has already examined the shipment of meat in question and ordered the entire shipment destroyed. So why in the world would I want to pay your blackmail, for your rotten meat?"

The attorney was speechless for a moment. He realized that the words "As I am sure you know" or "As I am sure you are aware of" often preceded the bombshell being dropped. Fegerson had used those very words himself, as he finished off his opponents in court. Fegerson had a sinking feeling that his air tight case he had carefully built was beginning to fall apart.

Howard added, "If you give me your mailing address, I will have my attorney forward you a copy of the government order."

Fegerson was sure he had taken care of everyone. For some men, it took just a small bribe; for others, it was as simple as threatening to fire them from their jobs. To Fegerson, justice was simply a matter of bribing the correct individual.

He had gotten to the union official with a case of T-Bone Steaks. He had offered the company attorney another case of T-Bone steaks for his testimony and a letter supporting Mexicali Meat Company. In thirty seconds of negotiation the matter on the phone, it had been agreed upon for fifty pounds of T-Bone Steaks and another fifty pound box of Rib-eye Steaks. The driver Samuel, and the meat inspector, Robert an employee of the meat company, had signed their sworn statements that Stevens had dictated to his secretary, without even reading them. Both men knew they would sign the statements or be fired on the spot. They had rent payments and car payments to make, so both men immediately signed what the attorney had typed up for them, as they did not want to lose their jobs.

Damn, Fegerson thought to himself, I thought I gotten to everyone. This was supposed to be as easy as stealing candy from a baby.

"What do you mean, the US government ordered the meats destroyed," Fegerson asked?

"Why don't you go up and see the ship's captain, and ask to see the log book. Why, I was sure you gentlemen would realize that with all that contaminated meat you delivered, I had no choice but to comply with the government order, or this ship could not come back into a US port."

Fegerson led the way up to the captain's office. Following along behind him were the union official and Jackson of Mexicali Meat Company. Asking the ship's captain to see the log book, the captain opened it to the section he realized that these men had come to see. There for all to see was written the following order:

By Order of the United States Customs:

The following cases of contaminated meat are refused entry into the United States, and shall be disposed of at sea beyond US territorial waters, or incinerated.

1. Case of meat, 52 pounds identified as # 2417

2. Case of meat, 47 pounds, identified as # 2418

3. Case of meat, 54 pounds, identified as # 2419

4. Case of meat, 46 pounds, identified as # 2420

5. Case of meat, 49 pounds, identified as # 2421

6. Case of meat, 52 pounds, identified as # 2422

7. Case of meat, 53 pounds, identified as # 1855

8. Case of meat, 51 pounds, identified as # 1856

9. Case of meat, 50 pounds, identified as # 1857

10. Case of meat, 48 pounds identified as # 1858

11. Case of meat, 52 pounds, identified as # 1859

12. Case of meat, 53 pounds, identified as # 1860

13. Case of meat, 51 pounds identified as # 147

14. Case of meat, 48 pounds, identified as # 145

The following cases of meat are refused entry into all US territorial waters, and jurisdictions and shall be destroyed, as they present a clear and present danger to public health and safety.

Signed: Michael Waite, Special Agent, United States Customs.

****

As they talked by the stern rail of the USS Sophie, Dancing Wind told Howard, "It has taken you a century, literally one hundred years, to correct your last mistake you made as a meat butcher in Chicago. *Do you know the rules, if you climb over the railing and commit suicide?*"

Howard was quiet as he listened to Dancing Wind.

"The rules are: you get to start all over again, for you will keep repeating the lessons you choose to learn, until you get them right! Do you really want to come back here again and relive every problem, difficulty and obstacle that you have already overcome?

"If you commit suicide now, when you get to heaven, you will find you will have to again come back here and experience the same lessons, again and again, until you learn them. See, the wonderful gift GOD has given you is free choice. You can learn your lessons in one lifetime, if that is your choice. Or you can relive the same lessons time and time again for thousands of years and dozens of life times if you are spiritually lazy or corrupt."

"You do not know everything about why I am planning to jump. My wife died of cancer. Then my son and daughter came home to help me out for the funeral. While there at the house, they took my wife's credit cards and charged up $30,000.00 on them. Literally, they maxed out all the credit cards. Then my son got my checkbook and savings account books out of the safe, and he has cleaned out all my savings and checking accounts. Literally all my life savings are gone! I have nothing. You would not believe it, but after working on this ship for three months, I planned to go back to my house. I went to the airport here in Hawaii and went to book a flight for the states. They told me my credit card was declined! I always pay my balance, whenever they send me a bill. I have it set up with the banks to pay it automatically.

"When I called the credit card company, they told me they canceled my cards after I failed to make any payments. They told me I still have to pay the bills anyway and I also owed them for three $5,000 cash advances I used. I never used the cash advance! Why even my cell phone has been canceled. I called the company and they told me they shut me off when I failed to pay the last two months of phone bills. They said I owe $2,871.00. I do not even make that much in a month working on this ship. I just left the airport and got back on this ship. What am I to do? I am totally broke, I cannot even fly home, as I am totally broke!"

"So, Howard, let's look at your problems and see if we can find some solutions, other than you taking a swim off the stern of this ship, which you will never return from. Are you committing suicide because your wife died of cancer?

Howard replied, "I guess not, but I have been very depresses about losing her. She was the best thing that ever happened to me. I love that woman."

"Do you think your wife (or husband—if it should apply to you) wants you to commit suicide just because they had their walking papers, taking them back to heaven," Dancing Wind asked?"

"No, I guess not", Howard replied. "She (he) always wanted the best for me. She (he) used to do small stuff all the time for me. Sometimes she (he) would make me my favorite dinner, or take me out to the restaurant they knew I liked. Sometimes we went to the movies and she (he) would let pick the movie even though I knew they wanted to see a different movie." He laughed, "GOD, I miss her (him)."

Dancing Wind told Howard, "It is perfectly natural and normal to miss someone you love. It comes with the territory of falling in love. I lost my own father to cancer. I still miss him. He was diagnosed with cancer and six months later, he was gone. In life there are the good times, as well as the times of tears. You're with the one you had, because you both loved each other. But I will tell you something about love you may not realize. It goes on beyond this life. For love transcends death.

"Your loved one will be waiting for you when it is your time to go *home*. And I know your wife (or husband–if appropriate) wants the best for you now, just as they would want you to open your heart and experience love again!

"For that is the very nature of love. It flows all around and about, where ever it is received, bringing GOD's blessing to all who let it into their hearts. GOD's love and grace is unlimited, it can fill your life, your lovers lives, a room, a house, a country, the world or thousands of worlds and it will never run out; it just takes spirits willing to let GOD's love flow in both their life and their actions. If you were to read about Jesus giving the Sermon on the Mount and his feeding of five thousand people, you would realize that Gods love was flowing around and through every word spoken by Jesus as well as everyone, as they experienced the miracle there."

Howard said, "What do I do about all my money? It's all gone! My credit rating is destroyed. I have lost everything!"

"You what?" Dancing Wind raised her voice and replied. "Did I just hear you say your money is everything? It is a mighty shallow person, a mighty stupid person, who thinks money is everything! A moment ago you were telling me your wife (husband), was the most important thing in your life. You still have some growing up to do!" the young teenager told the older man with white hair, standing beside her.

Howard leaned back and laughed. Never had he envisioned a teenager telling him he needed to grow up. But as he laughed at what she had said, he realized that anyone to whom money was everything, the end all, and the only thing which mattered, did indeed need to grow up.

"So, what is important?" he asked the Indian girl standing beside him with the black hair blowing across her face?

"Let's see what is important to you instead, ok? Is love important to you? Is completing your life purpose important? Is listening to your Guardian Angels important? Is being a human being, and helping those in need important? Is helping protect the environment and helping Mother Earth important? Howard, I cannot, no I will not, tell you what is important. I can only point out the options you have. In the end you must chose. For it is your life, a most precious life, and your decision to make, for GOD has given you free will to choose."

Howard asked, "What do I do about my credit cards, my money in the bank?"

Dancing Wind looked over the rail at the churning white water in the ships wake. "I can point out your two basic choices, and it is up to you. You have to choose. You can visit the police station and file a criminal report. The police will not get your money back, I am sorry but it is gone. The police will probable arrest your son and daughter. You will need to notify the credit card companies, immediately in writing that your credit cards have been stolen.

"The second option you have is to file bankruptcy. Then immediately close everything and start over. Open your bank accounts here on the islands, and start over. Your kids have burned you, they deliberately cheated you. Don't let them wipe you out financially again. I can assure you, what comes around goes around. So if they have not learned their lesson already, the next time will hit them like a sludge hammer. It is like time is speeding up, certainly karma is. So the actions they took and the reaction they have chosen to experience will hit them faster than ever before.

"You must protect yourself, so your children never hurt you again. You must make up completely new pass words on all your accounts. Don't facilitate your children in hurting you again. I am sorry, but you simply cannot trust them. You must also notify the three major credit bureaus that your identity has been stolen. Certainly you are not the first parent this has happened to, nor will you be the last. When you open new bank accounts chose completely new banks. Whichever course of action you choose to take; it is really your decision."

The sun was about to break on the eastern horizon. Daybreak had arrived. Howard asked Dancing Wind if he could hug her.

Dancing Wind nodded yes and smiled.

Howard hugged the teenager as tears ran down his face. "Thank you," he whispered in her ear. Holding her in his arms, out at arm's length he said, "I guess I have some thinking to do. I have some decisions I need to make. Young lady, you are certainly wise beyond your years."

The steward walked back inside the ship. He had his work day, as well as a whole new life ahead of him.

Dancing Wind slipped into her cabin. Molly was still asleep; slipping out of her clothes, she got under the covers and soon was fast asleep. Suddenly, only fifteen minutes later, a pillow hit Dancing Wind twice in the head.

Molly said, "Get up sleepy head, it is time for breakfast."

The Guardian Angel spoke to the spirit
In my hand I hold five treasures
Show me now insisted the spirit
For he had been trying to achieve wealth for a lifetime.
In one hand the Angel held
Gold, Silver, Diamonds, Sapphires and Rubies.
In the other hand the Angel held:
Friendship, Loyalty, Trust, Companionship, and Love.
Turning to the spirit, the Angel said:
Choose which ever hand you want most.
The Spirit immediately reached for the hand containing the
Gold, Silver, Diamonds, Sapphires and Rubies.
The Angel accepted the Spirits choice,
As he had for over twenty five thousand years, times three.
The Angel had been offering the Spirit
Friendship, Loyalty, Trust, Companionship and Love
Just as your Guardian Angel has been offering these gifts to you
for over twenty five thousands years, times three.

Solo

(Six trips up onto Frenchman Mountain)

A hint of spring was in the air. The days were becoming longer with the change to daylight savings time. The days were growing warmer though the nights still had a cold chill in the air. The green grass was peeking out of the taller dry brown plants from the previous year. The geese flocks were beginning to fly north, yet the high mountains were still white with their winter snow.

It was on such a day that Dancing Wind and her Indian teacher, Dan had come to park their car in the parking area by the bridge crossing the Rio Grande on Paseo del Norte. For like the restless river flowing beside the walking paths; Dan saw the restlessness in Dancing Wind and her impatience to be tracking the old trails in the high mountains. The trails they would track as they walked along the dirt paths in the Bosque were not to be seen in foot prints in the ground but the path of the thoughts in the mind. For the wise old teacher had seen the questions forming in his students mine so he thought a quiet walk along the river would help her relax and calm her mind. Then as they walked he was sure, as sun rise follows the night, the questions would come.

Dancing Wind walked on the dirt path beside her dear friend Dan. They walked in silence just enjoying each other's company as dear friends can.

Dan turned to Dancing Wind and said, "When are you going to track the trail up on Frenchman Mountain?"

Dancing Wind replied, "I was hoping for company. I asked the man from Utah if he would accompany me and he backed out at the last minute saying his wife and kids were sick. Since then I have not heard from him in several months. So next I invited a man from Oklahoma and he was unable to come as his roof leaked so he had to put a new roof on his business. Then I invited the man from South Carolina and he too was unable to make it. Finally I invited the experienced prospector from Colorado and he too was unable to come as he could not get off work."

Dan turned to Dancing Wind and replied, "How many times does it take for you to realize the trail was intended for you to track by yourself? This is a solo trail for you to track, as the lessons are for you. If you do not track this trail shortly; then your Guardian Angels will release this trail and it's lessons to another."

"Do you want to go with me?"

Dan replied, "Well that is an idea." And he stopped to clean his pipe and pack it with tobacco and then lite it. They continued walking in silence as Dan said nothing more.

Dancing Wind realized that there was not an answer from Dan and she did not want to push for a reply she felt would be negative so she said, "Well just think about it."

Dan replied, "You know that there are some trails you should not track at all, you need to walk away from them. These trails, all you can do is put them in your prayers. Now these are not the trails I speak to you about now. I am speaking now of the trails that a tracker like you is fully capable of tracking. There are some trails you can track with friends, there are some trails you can only track with experienced trackers who will stand by you to the limit of their existence. And then there are the trails you need to track by yourself as they have lessons you need to learn, understand the lesson it teaches you, and incorporate that learning into your life experience.

"The trail upon Frenchman Mountain is a trail both your Guardian Angel and I feel you should track as it is an excellent learning experience for you. There are three trails up upon that mountain. I suggest you listen to your Guardian Angels counsel and pick one of the trails to track. Then go all the way and track it to completion. If you fail to track it this year, the only person who will lose out on the lessons is the person you see in the mirror every day. Certainly tracking the trail from 1804 up upon Frenchman Mountain is easier than taking an Algebra 2 class for you, and it will be a lot more applicable to your life right now."

Later that month, Dancing Wind traveled to Frenchmen Mountain to get a feel for the trail she reluctantly felt she should track. On the West side of the mountain were numerous signs posted "No Trespassing" where ever she looked. There appeared to be four ways in. The more difficult route would take her up the seep north face of the mountain. While the southern route had a road clearly marked "No Trespassing." This second route would take her to the southern slope of the mountain; while longer than the north slope, it seemed to be the more gradual of a slope and easier climb getting up and down the mountain.

The third way she saw on a map was a road going towards the center portion of the mountain on the east side of the mountain. She decided to check out this route last.

The map showed her there was a fourth way into the mountains which was through some state lands on the south east side of the mountain. When she went over to investigate this route in she found the private land owners had posted every access point with "No Trespassing" signs. Certainly getting into these mountains was proving difficult. For two days Dancing Wind tried to find a way into the mountains where she would simply be left alone.

When Dancing Wind left the mountains she just had pictures of the various ways in. None of the ways were going to be easy. Nor did it look like any of the ways in would be legal. Dancing Wind figured she would have to slip into and off of the mountain without ever being seen. Certainly tracking a trail on Frenchman Mountain was certainly going to be a challenge.

Dancing Winds second trip to Frenchman Mountain occurred in May when the flowers were beginning to open and the green grass was peeking out behind last year's dead brown grass. Early in the morning she packed her backpack with a lunch, two bottles of water, her camera, Global Positioning System (GPS), two spare batteries for the GPS, a tiny saw, toilet paper, knife, matches, magnesium fire starter, a small folding saw, compass, a topo map of the mountain and her Glock with a spare magazine.

For Dancing Wind this trip up upon Frenchman Mountain was really just a scouting trip to give her a feel for the mountain and she also planned to take her camera for photos. At seven am Dancing Wind began climbing the South east corner of Frenchmen Mountain. The sun was out and it looked like a beautiful day. She wore a jacket as the morning was chilly but she figured by noon she would have it tied behind her backpack as the day warmed up.

About eleven, Dancing Wind had removed her jacket and was taking pictures from the top of the mountain she had climbed. As Dancing Wind climbed the southern slopes she caught hints of the trail she was tracking. She could feel the hunger of the men, she knew they were not far from starvation. She also sensed the fear. She realized the fear was decreasing as the men climbed higher on the bare mountain slopes for they felt that their rifles gave them an advantage over the Indians trying to kill them. At least while on this mountains they knew they would not be ambushed by the Indians. But there was a feeling desperation all around her she could feel their concern about the black powder for their rifles was almost gone. There was the feeling of the loss of so many of their friends to ambushes by hostile Indians as well as an equal number had died from starvation and sickness brought on my malnutrition. Many of the men felt they had been abandoned by their country (France) and the promised supplies they had so desperately needed had never arrived. As Dancing Wind walked among the slate gray mountain slopes it was as if the spirits upon the mountain were sharing their innermost thoughts with her.

Suddenly Dancing Winds Guardian Angel Lily interrupted her thought with a warning; a very strong warning that danger was approaching. Dancing Wind immediately reinforced her White Light of Protection around herself and then open her senses and intuition to the source of the danger. While she was scanning the terrain for possible sources of danger she suddenly realized she was shivering from cold. She untied her jacket from her backpack and slipped it on and zipped the jacket up. Then she felt a cold wind pick up as the dark gray clouds blocked out the sun. While she had been tracking the trails and paying attention to the early trail up upon the mountain top she had failed to realize a sudden shift in the weather.

Dancing Wind spoke with Lily her Guardian Angel, and was advised to get off the mountain now as the weather was deteriorating rapidly. Suddenly big fat rain drops started splattering upon her face and the wind rose in intensity. Within minutes she could hear the winds howling and whistling in the scattered pine trees. Dancing Wind reached into her pack and pulled out her GPS to look for the shortest route back to her jeep. She held the unit up in the sky allowing it time to lock onto the satellites traveling over head in orbit out

246 • Barton R Thom

in space. It seemed the unit was taking forever to give her a position.

Then the full force of the cold front which brought in the storm hit her. The rain started coming down in sheets of water carried by the force of the wind. Glancing at her GPS she knew she had to get moving as soon as she got the directions back to her car. Instead the GPS simply said "Low Battery." Then it shut itself off.

Immediately Dancing Wind reached into her pack and pulled out her two spare AA batteries. As she removed the two dead batteries and prepared to install the new pair, a bolt of lightning crashed into the mountain top not eight hundred feet away. Dancing Wind jumped in fright and the two spare batteries went flying from her hand. Somewhere in the loose rocks her only new batteries had disappeared.

There was nothing left to do but put the nonworking GPS in her pack. Dancing Wind began walking following the contour line she was on as she began walking around the mountain towards her car. Around her the storm intensified and she struggled to see even a hundred feet in the intense rain. For hours she walked and then she realized she was completely lost.

Her shoes squeaked as she walked. She could feel her toes freezing as she felt the water squishing with every step. Then she felt rain water running down her back on the inside of her jacket as it became totally saturated with water. Dancing Wind realized she had to find shelter as soon as possible or she could die from exposure.

As she walked she decided to gradually drop in elevation while she looked for shelter or a place to build a fire. In the time it took to drop five hundred feet in elevation she realized her teeth had begun to chatter on their own. She was not sure she could feel her toes. And then as if Mother Nature was making one last effort to show that winter was not quite over the blowing rain turned to snow!

In twenty minutes the slate gray rocky ground began turning white as the Snow Pixies made their snowflakes. The snow proved to be a blessing for Dancing Wind as the visibility increased to about two hundred feet and she was able to see a dead pine tree further down the hill. Immediately Dancing Wind altered her direction of travel and headed straight for the tree, for she knew she must built a fire or she would die of exposure on this mountain. She no longer had control of her teeth as they involuntary chattered and she had fits of shivers run through her body.

When she reached the dead tree Dancing Wind immediately began removing the smaller branches and limbs and these she placed in a sheltered location out of the wind. Here she would build her fire. Making a small tepi of small sticks she then removed her knife and a magnesium bar from her pack. Next she began shaving thin shaving of magnesium on the wet wood and in the center of her tipi of wood. Then she took a wood match and placed the burning match up against the magnesium shavings. They immediately caught fire giving off a white hot flame. Quickly her little wooden tipi was engulfed in flames and she began adding larger sticks and smaller limbs to build up her fire to warm herself. Throughout the night Dancing Wind kept the fire burning as the snow swirled in the wind and fell about her. Gradually she began to warm up and she would put an item of clothing near the fire on a branch to try and dry it as much as possible.

Unknown to Dancing Wind about six hundred feet away another small fire burned. There an old Lakota Indian warmed himself by his fire as he drank a cup of hot coffee and smoked his pipe. The lines on his weather face revealed his age. That he was here on this mountain reflected his concern for the teenage girl he watched over. Thought Dancing Wind never saw her tracking teacher he was there watching over her. Dan would just watch as long as Dancing Wind was in no serious danger.

In the morning Dancing Wind climbed down off Frenchmen Mountain, while the top of the mountain was a beautiful white covered in snow, at the base of the mountain two thousand feet lower there was no snow on the ground at all. Dancing Wind decided it was just a case of bad luck getting caught in a early Spring Snow storm in the Rocky Mountains. Though next time she resolved to bring rain gear she could put over her jacket and to carry a couple of extra double A batteries.

When Dancing Wind returned to Albuquerque to see Dan, he asked her to tell him all about her trip. She told how her tracking was going fine until a bad storm came up. It rained and snowed and she had to build a fire to keep from freezing. Dan asked the questions any concerned person would ask.

Then Dan asked her about her tracking and he asked her what she had learned. Dancing Wind told her tracking teacher that she had picked up bits and pieces of the old trail going up the south slope of the mountain. She told Dan her initial impressions were, it was a French trail and the men had been in desperate straits. Most of the men in their expedition had died of sickness brought upon by malnutrition—they were starving. A large number had died in Indian ambushes.

Dan suggested that, on her next trip, Dancing Wind take up food and water and leave if for the spirits. "You want to begin working with them and gaining their confidence and trust. You can also start including them in your prayers. Talk with the spirits and interact with them as long as they show you dignity, honor and integrity. It may be that you will be able to help each other. In an ideal situation you both work together and help each other and everyone can walk away from the experience as a winner.

"So, how many spirits are on the mountain in the area you were in?"

"I don't know, but I will talk with them more next time I go there and I will find out"

"Find out if there is there anything the spirits would like your help with or that you can do to help them."

"The first step I will do when I return is take them food and water and leave it there for them."

Dan asked, "Have you considered the salt?"

"No, what are you talking about?"

"Well, on your next trip up to Frenchmen Mountain, keep salt in the back of your mind.

"You should also learn if the spirits are willing to help you recovery any possible treasure located there. You have taken the first step by beginning to communicate with them and learning about the conditions which drove them to seek shelter upon the mountain.

"Keep in mind, though, that the loyalty of these men lies with France. When they were exploring these Rocky Mountains this was in the Louisiana territory and it belonged to France.

"Just remember, you cannot let yourself promise to give a gift to a specific person or church which existed in 1798 as the church may not exist anymore. Certainly a person living in 1798 would be difficult for you to find and deliver a gift to. So carefully watch how you give your word. For once you give your word you are obligated to carry it out.

****The Third Trip Up Upon Frenchmen Mountain****

In late June, Dancing Wind again returned to Frenchman Mountain. This time she brought a small tent, sleeping bag and a backpack with supplies for staying overnight. Around a campfire that evening, Dancing Wind invited the spirits of the Frenchmen to join her. As each spirit joined her around her camp fire she poured them water in small paper cups and she set cheese, crackers and jerky in front of them. Giving the spirits food was a courtesy and it is always polite to offer spirits food.

As the spirits joined her at the fire she invited them to help themselves. There were five Frenchmen who came up and sat around the fire with her. One of the spirits, Jean wiped tears from his eyes as he cried. Never had any one offered them food in over two hundred years. The gift was especially appropriate as they had been starving and so many had died from malnutrition.

Dancing Wind introduced herself and told them she came from southwest of there at Abiquiu, New Mexico. Then she asked each of them in turn their names, their occupation and where they were from. Batista was the first spirit whom spoke with her. He was a wrangler skilled in handling mules. He had come down from Montreal, Canada. Pierre-Louis was a hunter who hunted providing the group with buffalo, deer, elk and occasionally mountain sheep for meals. In Canada he had been a Voyager working for the

Hudson Bay Company as a trapper. Both men had died in ambushes by Ute Indians. Masse was a carpenter who had worked constructing their living quarters, and built sluice boxes for placer mining said he died of cholera from bad water.

Massie was from an area just north of New Orleans in Louisiana. Jean was a soldier with the French but he pretended to be a civilian merchant clerk to avoid difficulties with the Spanish officials in New Orleans. Jean said he had starved in the winter of 1799 as he was snowed in at their high mountain camp near Treasure Mountain. While with hindsight he thought his starvation could have been avoided by leaving the high mountains for a lower elevation, he thought his starvation was a result of not realizing that all the game would leave the high elevations before the winter snow hit.

Once the winter snows hit the high San Juan Mountains he was trapped in a mountain valley with no wild game and no way out. Jacques had come from France and then down from Montréal. He had come on a flat boat to New Orleans where the logs from the flat boat were sold to make lumber. Jacques said he was a miner and he died as a result of a bad cough he developed which would not go away, when winter came and food became very scarce he caught a cold and passed away in his sleep. This expedition by the French was intended to provided him with the money to buy himself land and build him a house near his home town of La Harve, France.

Since the French government was in turmoil in 1800 and their Louisiana territory was far from France, the French expedition exploring and mapping their new lands was basically forgotten or overlooked when it came to sending a ship from France on a regular basis and getting supplies to their expedition of exploration. In theory it took six months from the moment the French government decided to ship supplies to the French Explores in the Rocky Mountains to receive any thing shipped from France.

The loading of the ship and sailing to New Orleans took three months and then loading up the supplies and shipping them from New Orleans to the Rocky mountains required another three months. That is in theory, involve the government decision making process, the allocation of funds to purchase supplies, the political infighting over where money is spent, the need to fully load the cargo ship before sailing, the clearing of customs purchasing mules in New Orleans and hiring wranglers and packers to move the supplies out on the frontier and then at least a year was needed to get any supplies to their explores in the Rocky Mountains. While the men in the expedition had been promised supplies the limited supplies they received initially were meager at best and nonexistent by the end in 1803-1804. Had the expedition received the provisions they required the Rocky Mountains today might have remained French. Certainly the French government would not have been selling the rich mineral resources of Colorado for three cents an acre.

The stories of the French mining gold and silver in Colorado many years prior to our own Louis and Clark expedition of exploration are true. The ruins of their main headquarters can be found in the San Louis Valley. The stone foundations show the buildings were about 60 feet long and thirty feet wide.** Unfortunately the French Expedition which was charged with mapping, exploration and mining suffered staggering losses due to starvation, disease and hostile Indian attacks. Originally they numbered about 300 men in 1799. By about 1804 there were less than 100 men left and only a handful of these men made it back to France alive.

The men whom Dancing Wind encountered upon Frenchman Mountain were five spirits who had died, yet they still followed the last few survivors of the expedition to Frenchman Mountain where they decided to cache a small portion of the gold and silver they had mined in the Rocky Mountains. Then the surviving French men left the mountain headed towards the Arkansas River and followed it east towards Saint Louis. These five spirits Dancing Wind encountered chose to remain upon the mountain and guard the treasure they had given their lives to obtain.

France had sent a 300-man expedition exploring the Louisiana territory and exploring the Rocky Mountains looking for mineral wealth. This expedition was an expedition to explore Frances new territory and assess its potential for providing resources valuable back in France. Specifically they were charged with mapping the Louisiana territory and reporting on all natural and mineral resources. Near the site of Treasure Mountain the French explores had discovered rich silver deposits with smaller deposits of gold.

They had been far from any civilized outpost so mostly they had to rely on the wild game they hunted. But feeding 300 men in winter was not an easy job. Originally all the supplies they carried west came from Saint Louis, Missouri and New Orleans, both located on the Mississippi River. Only what supplies the mules could carry came west with them. After a year living in the Rocky Mountains all the supplies they had originally brought west were completely exhausted. Some supplies were obtained from Abiquiu and Taos in the Spanish territory to the south.

They had been promised a pack train of supplies in the fall which would have helped the expedition get through the severe Rocky Mountain winters but these pack trains of supplies were never sent. As a result, many of the men died from malnutrition or sickness brought on by malnutrition.

The last thirty survivors of the three hundred man French expedition were fighting their way back to New Orleans when they sought the safety of French Man Mountain. Here they decided to lighten the load the mules carried so that they could make better time. Having crossed the pass to the south west of them their intended path of travel would take them to the northerly branch of the Taos Trail where it lead to the Arkansas River.

They planned to follow the river east towards New Orleans. Unfortunately they had encountered scattered ambushes by Ute Indians and lost many men and their riding horses so five of the French men were afoot. If they were to keep up with the rest of their countrymen they too needed to ride. They reluctantly decided to cache five mule loads of gold and silver up upon this mountain.

The gentle slope of the mountain on the south side allowed the men to ride their horses and mules up the mountain. Because the mountain was mostly rocky with only scattered trees it would allow the Frenchmen to see any Indians approaching them. With the gold and silver cached the men without horses had the mules they could ride so they could all travel faster.

The five spirits remained on the mountain as they were held earth bound as spirits or ghost as they were unwilling to go *home* as the buried treasure represented everything they had worked for to obtain and died trying to protect. Yet as spirits they were unable to move a single gold or silver bar or spent their treasure. Their dreams of living a life of wealth was something they still dreamed of. Yet part of them realized it was not to be. The attachment for the treasure held them there on Frenchman Mountain for over two centuries.

Over the years, different trackers had occasionally come to Frenchman Mountain and followed the trail to the cache of buried gold and silver. The first trackers had removed the gold bars. Not being greedy or taking more than they needed the five mule loads of treasure had slowly decreased from repeatedly withdraws made over the centuries until now all that remained was half a mule load, literally one pannier of silver finger bars. This was the treasure Dancing Wind sought.

To help Dancing Wind locate the treasure she had asked the assistance of the five spirits still living upon the mountain. Dancing Wind asked them for their help and in return for their assistance she promised them she would donate 25% of what she recovered to the churches and help feed the hungry in Attakapas Post, Louisiana and Montréal, Canada.

They in turn told her they would all stand together as a group over the treasure site so she could film it with her camera. On her film Dancing Wind hoped to capture the images of the five spirits and additionally the location of the buried treasure.

Using a camera Dancing Wind asked the Spirits to stand over the treasure cache site and then she would use the camera to capture a picture of the spirits in reference to the terrain. Then she would be able to simply examine her photos and then walk to the site of the treasure cache.

To catch the spirits on film, Dancing Wind told the Spirits she planned to take photos at the crack of dawn, at noon and then in the evening. She was not sure which time period would best capture the images she sought. At the end of the day Dancing Wind left the mountain with a hundred pictures which she could examine at her leisure at home in Abiquiu.

After examining her photos and selecting the five best photos showing where the French Spirits stood upon the mountain, Dancing Wind took these to a photography shop and had five large prints made which she could carry in her back pack back up upon the mountain. These were for her to examine upon the mountain top so she could insure she was at the exact spot the spirits had stood so she would know exactly where to dig for the treasure.

****The fourth Trip up Frenchman Mountain****

Dancing Wind had to be patient as the next planned trip back to Frenchman mountain had to be postponed due to a storm front moving East out of California. Two weeks later, Dancing Wind climbed Frenchman Mountain this time her pack also contained a metal detector and a pick /mattock for digging. Upon reaching the top of the mountain Dancing Wind used the photos of the spirits to locate the area to search with her Pulse Induction metal detector.

As Dancing Wind believed the silver was buried less than four feet deep, she did not bring her large five-by-five-foot search coil, and instead she brought a smaller one that measured three by three feet. After assembling her search coil she searched the possible location and in twenty minutes she had located the best spot to dig. Using her pick and mattock she loosed the dirt and stones with the pick and scraped a little dirt and a lot of rocks away with the mattock. In forty five minutes she was four feet deep when she swing her pick and it clearly hit metal.

Clearing away the rocks in the hole Dancing Wind saw three tiny bars of silver. Each bar of silver was about one inch by one inch by twelve inches long. All three bars were black from tarnish over the years except for the bar she had struck with her pick. That part had a shiny spot showing a bright silver where Dancing Winds pick had scratched the metal surface. Dancing Wind was delighted with her discovery. Then she turned and thanked the five spirits she had worked with. Resuming her digging the teenager expanded and deepened her hole to recover more of the silver bars. In thirty minutes more digging she had uncovered fourteen bars of the Frenchmen's silver.

Removing all the bars from the hole she carefully scanned the hole with the metal detector. This scan was just to ensure there was nothing else in the hole. Then Dancing Wind partially filled in the hole with the rocks and dirt. When the hole was only a foot deep she stopped filling in the hole and began returning the silver bars to the shallow hole.

Laying the bars two high, Dancing Wind returned nine silver bars back into the hole and covered them up under about eight inches of loose dirt and rocks. The five silver bars went into her pack. Then Dancing Wind packed up her metal detector and the digging tool in her back pack and taking a moment to drink some water she then hiked down off the mountain to her jeep.

****The fifth trip upon Frenchman Mountain****

That night, Dancing Wind examined the silver bars. They were unique, having the Crest of France indented into the bars surface. Before turning in for the night Dancing Wind buried the silver bars below her campfire site.

Then next morning Dancing Wind again hiked up to the location of the buried silver. On this trip ,Dancing Wind did not take her metal detector, she did not need it as he knew exactly where the silver was buried. Nor did she take her digging tool. Instead in her pack she carried a block of salt for the Mountain Sheep she had seen grazing on the mountain. Finding a location to place the salt block where the mountain sheep would not be exposed to prying eyes Dancing Wind left the salt block in a grove of Colorado Blue Spruce trees.

Then Dancing Wind went over to the cache of silver bars and removed five more silver bars which she placed in her back pack. Then she again hiked down off the mountain. In her camp Dancing Wind again buried the silver below her campfire circle. She now had ten bars of silver.

****The sixth Trip up Frenchman Mountain****

The following morning, Dancing Wind again hiked up the mountain to the site of the silver cache. Opening the hole she removed two of the last four bars of silver. Then she began filling the hole in. The French man, Jacquez then turned to Dancing Wind and asked her if she wasn't forgetting something as he looked at the two bars of silver in the hole.

Dancing Wind kiddingly replied, "You're right," as she softly hit her forehead with her hand.

Turning, Dancing Wind reached into her pack and removed a bag containing some red clover and some sacred corn. In the hole where the two bars of silver lie the teenager scattered some Hopi Pink corn and then she finished filling in the hole. Around her she broad cast the red clover seeds to help the nature spirits. Then she thanked the nature spirits.

Turning to the French spirits, she said, "Follow me" as she started down off the mountain. Massie looked back at the location where the hole had been, there really was no reason for them to stay upon Frenchmen Mountain any longer. If the teenage girl could walk away from the two silver bars, showing she was not controlled by greed, and having to take it all, well then they realized they could too.

A month later, Dancing Wind was in the Louisiana Parish of St Martin. Here at St. Martinville, she entered the St Martin de Tours Catholic Church. Walking through the doors she dropped to one knee as she entered the church and using her right hand made the sign of the Cross. Beside her the five Frenchmen's spirits also dropped to their knees and followed her example.

Then she walked up to the altar and set a donation on it. Then she turned to Batista, Massie, Jean, Jacquez, and Pierre-Louis and asked, "Have I kept my word to you?"

Jean said, "I also wanted a donation to feed the poor."

Dancing Wind replied, "We will go there next." And so they did.

After making a donation to a food bank, Dancing Wind looked around and noticed she still had the company of all five Frenchmen. Yet Dancing Wind was unconcerned about helping the spirits return *home,* as the two major challenges had already been successfully passed back in Colorado when she had been able to interact with the Frenchmen, and get them to have a purpose other than sitting up upon the mountain. By getting them to think outside themselves and think of helping others half the battle in taking them *home* had already been won.

The second half of the battle was when the spirits followed her off the mountain she had gotten the spirits to travel. From experience Dancing Wind knew that a spirits that travel are always easier to take home than spirits which will not budge from a location, or will not interact with you in any manner.

And so, by getting the spirits to accompany her off the mountain, Dancing Wind considered the second half of the battle already won. All she had to do now was ensure every spirit was present and aware at the moment she kept her promise to them. By calling them in or engaging them in conversation she was sure she had the spirits attention at the moments she was keeping her promise to each of them.

Two weeks later, Dancing Wind was up in Buffalo, New York. There she crossed the border into Canada. Her Destination was Montreal, Canada. As she drove north on the highway she passed a small town of Grimsby, Ontario. There in Canada's banana belt fruit tree orchards grew along both sides of the highway, and the tears began to flow down her cheeks.

Jacquez turned to the teenage girl beside him and said, "It will be Ok, Missie." For Jacquez could feel the despair and anguish Dancing Wind felt at the slaughter of so many Americans and French which had occurred here centuries earlier.

Dancing Wind realized that the trail upon Frenchman Mountain was now taking her upon another trail she would have to track in Grimsby, Ontario. Yet for now she would follow Dan's counsel and only track one trail at a time. When she had completed her work on tracking the trail upon Frenchman Mountain she would then be free to track another trail.

In Montreal there is an old French Church known as Notre Dame Basilica and it was here on rue Notre Dame oust that she was accompanied by Batista, Massie, Jacquez, Pierre-Louis and Jean. As Dancing Wind entered the church she moved ten feet through the doors before dropping to one knee and using her right hand she made the sign of the cross. Behind her, five Frenchmen followed her example.

As she looked up, the church took her breath away it was simply so beautiful. The main colors inside this magnificent church were blue. Never had she seen such a beautiful church with such beautiful harmony of colors and the high arched ceilings. Getting up, Dancing Wind walked up to the altar and made a donation in the offering plate. Then she walked back to the church pews and sat down.

Turning to the five spirits in the pew behind her she asked, "Have I kept my word to you?"

The five spirits all replied, "Yes."

Then Dancing Wind got down on her knees and began saying the "Lord's Prayer" as she was saying the prayer to GOD, somewhere in the back of her mind she through it strange, as it was as if dozens of people were also saying the "Lord's Prayer" along with her.

What she thought was strange was the church had very few people inside it now, and none near her, yet it was as if dozens of men were saying the prayer along with her and all of them were speaking in Latin. In Montreal, she expected to hear French, but not Latin.

When she finished the prayer Dancing Wind stood up and looked around to see where all the people had come from that she had heard praying. Dancing Wind was by herself, for no one else was close by her pew. The five Frenchmen had also gone *home* while she was in prayer. She wondered if the French men she had accompanied into the church spoke French yet prayed in Latin.

As Dancing Wind walked out of the tall wooden doors of Notre Dame Basilica and started down the stone steps, suddenly a wide smile appeared upon her face as she saw the weathered face of a dear friend. For there, getting up from where he was sitting, stood her best friend Dan.

"Can I buy you lunch?" he asked. "You can tell me about your solo journey, what adventures you encountered and what you learned."

The friendship between a spirit tracker and a student is a close one. At times their thoughts may actually be as one. For the teacher wants their student tracker to succeed as much or, sometimes, even more so, than the student. As a Lakota medicine man, Dan knew where the trails would lead Dancing Wind, as she spirit tracked the trails of the French explores. He hoped Dancing Wind would be able to take the last of the spirits home for that was the second most important outcome of tracking the trail.

While Dan felt that Dancing Wind needed to track this trail by herself, the most important outcome was ensuring his student was safe, so he occasionally looked in upon Dancing Wind as she tracked a trail through time, to achieve the best possible outcome, and that is what real friends do.

**Source: Maynard Cornett Adams—"Citadel Mountain 1"

Angels give guidance
Angels give Love
Listen to your Angel
For guidance from Above

Path of the Angels

Sometimes you think you have an idea or plan of what you are going to do, like look for Spanish markers, or locate an old Spanish treasure, but your Guardian Angels may have plans of their own. You think you are in charge, and so you have let your Guardian Angels know what you are searching for, yet the Guardian Angels may have their own ideas of what you should be doing. Such was the case on the day that Dancing Wind followed the Path of the Angels.

The morning started with both the teenager Dancing Wind, and her wise old tracking teacher Dan, packing their backpacks for a long difficult hike through the mountains. They packed water, a lunch, toilet paper, a tiny three inch shovel to bury their toilet paper, matches, a magnesium fire starter, knife, compass, G.P.S. (a satellite global positioning system), a map, a camera and a handgun for self-defense. The most important item to pack is water because in the desert southwest to travel far or fast, water is absolutely essential.

The climb up the mountain was a difficult climb because the steep slopes were of loose sand. So for every three steps up the mountain, they slid back down one step. Long before the sun had risen enough to cast sunlight on the slopes, the two trackers were stopping to rest and drink some of their cold water. They had packed four bottles of water each. The night before, they had prepared the bottles of water by placing them in the freezer to allow them to freeze solid. In the morning, they placed the frozen water bottles in their backpacks so even as the summer heat climbed into the 80's F they would have cold water to drink throughout the day.

Dancing Wind's Guardian Angel Lily led the way up the steep mountain slopes. She was followed by Dancing Wind who was in turn followed by Dan who was teaching Dancing Wind to track in the spirit realm. Though Dan was more experienced, he let Dancing Wind lead the way, because a student should not follow the teacher, but should put into practice the lessons he taught.

At a cut indentation in the mountain slope, about ten feet high and a hundred feet long, Lily stopped to allow stopped to allow Dancing Wind and Dan time to look over the site. While the vegetation was typical of the other parts of the mountain slope, the cut into the mountain was definitely man made. Had you asked Dancing Wind when the cut was made, she would have told you about 1850-1860. The date would have come from her Guardian Angel, Lily without her consciously realizing it.

She also realized that there was a man-made door located near the center of the cut. When she walked past the hidden stone door, she felt it give off a bad vibration, as well as causing her stomach to feel upset. She had learned these feelings were signs warning her of danger and knew she must leave the door alone.

Lily told her, *"Do not touch it!"*

She knew, if she dug down about seven feet, there would be a man-made door centuries old, but she also realized that there would likely be a lightning bolt or a broken red heart on or beside the door warning of the death to come to anyone trying to enter the old Spanish death trap. With this understanding, she ignored the false trail and continued moving on up the slope of the mountain looking for the trail to the actual treasure site.

One hundred yards further up the slope, she stopped to look over the jaws of the trap which would spring upon anyone foolish enough to try and open the stone door down below.

Trigger Stone on a Spanish Death Trap

There, poised on the slope of the cliff, was a ten-ton flat surface slider death trap rock that would slide down the slope extremely rapidly. A single six-inch stone trigger held the huge boulder in place. If the trap was tripped, releasing the trigger stone, then the ten ton stone would be sent flying down the slope. Another ten tons of smaller boulders would be knocked loose and follow the big flat slider stone down to bury any one foolish enough to open the stone door directly below it. Probably a channel of sand was run between the huge flat surface slider rock and the door below so that when the door was open, the sand would pour through the doorway releasing the trigger stone. Moments later the flat surface slider

Death Trap Rock would arrive to kill the intruders who opened the door!

Continuing on up the slope, Dancing Wind encountered a couple of more Spanish markers, a compass stone giving directions and a shadow marker of a Saguaro cactus and a couple of shadow arrows about ten feet long. A short time later she had reached the top of the mountain, only it was not a mountain at all but the top of Mesa de Abiquiu. Before her were hundreds of acres covered in piñon (pine) and cedar trees with patches of grassy meadows among the trees.

Dancing Wind sat down with Dan and took a break to eat some fruit, and drink some water. Dancing Wind turned to Lily and asked her if she would like some water.

Lily joking replied, "No thank you. I have to watch my figure."

After they had eaten and rested, she asked Dan what he thought they should do.

Dan replied, "It is your show."

As Dancing Wind started to get up and her back was turned to Dan and Lily, Dan winked to Lily, for clearly Dan realized what the Angel was up to.

So Lily led the way across the mesa to the northwest followed by Dancing Wind, with Dan following behind. Through the trees on a wandering path Lily walked as she kept up a steady conversation with Dancing Wind. As long as she knew Dancing Wind's attention was focused upon her, she would continue walking towards the site she intended. Had

Dancing Wind's attention lapsed she would have instantly changed direction away from the approaching danger.

A half hour later, they walked into a large meadow. Dancing Wind's Guardian Angel told her that this used to be a large Indian camp over a century ago. Dan hung back as they entered the site of the Indian village as he did not want to distract Dancing Wind from her conversation with Lily. For Dan realized that Lily was teaching Dancing Wind a dangerous spiritual lesson.

Lily had her own plans for today and they had nothing to do with looking for Spanish treasure. Lily was intent on teaching the teenager tracker two lessons. The first lesson was to recognize a serious danger when it appeared. The second lesson was to recover a treasure far more dear and precious to Lily than a hand full of gold bars.

As Dancing Wind explored the site of the Indian village, her Guardian Angel pointed out to both of them where the tipi lodges were located as well as where the village obtained its water. The spring which long ago had provided an abundance of water for the Indians was now dry. The violence against nature and the violence of man against man had so upset the water spirits that they had withdrawn their energy and life giving water. Where once a small stream had flowed was now just a dry dusty watercourse.

Then, Dancing Wind saw the spirit/ghost of a man to the east of her. His back was turned to her, and when he knew that she had seen him, he slowly started to walk away from the Indian village and traveled at a slow walk to the southeast on Mesa de Abiquiu. He was slowly walking to the southeast to enable Dancing Wind to easily follow him. Walking out of the Indian village, Dancing Wind began following the spirit. Tagging along beside Dancing Wind was her Guardian Angels. Dan followed along behind them.

Lily turned to Dancing Wind and asked her a question. "Why is the spirit keeping his back to you? Would not a friendly spirit come up and introduce himself?"

Dancing Wind, stopped as if lost in thought, as she considered the question Lily had asked her. Certainly Lily's question had a reason behind it.

Lily glanced at Dan with a question in her eyes. "Was she handling this lesson OK?"

Dan nodded, reassuring to Lily she was handling the situation just fine.

When Dancing Wind lost sight of the spirit, he would always stop to allow her to see him, so she would not lose the trail as he lured her away from the Indian village.

Dancing Wind started to follow the spirit for another fifty feet.

She glanced back at Dan.

Dan said nothing, giving Dancing Wind time to think.

She followed the spirit another twenty-five feet.

She glanced at Lily. Lily asked Dancing Wind, "Is he acting like a friend?"

The spirit would never turn and face Dancing Wind as he led her further and further away from the village. Rapidly Dancing Wind's apprehension grew more and more until she would follow the spirit no more! For Dancing Wind realized the spirit was leading her into his trap! Promptly Dancing Wind stopped following the Spirit and she told him in a loud clear and commanding voice: "I WILL NOT FOLLOW YOU ANOTHER STEP UNLESS YOU TURN AROUND AND FACE ME SO I CAN SEE YOU CLEARLY. THEN TELL ME ALL YOUR NAMES!"

Lily knew that Dancing Wind wanted to see the spirit's face to see if she recognized him. By looking into his face she not only expected to see if he was an honest man or an evil spirit but she also wanted to see his aura, the light around his body, to help her tell if he was telling her a lie. By insisting he tell her all his names, she was not allowing him to tell her one alias she would not recognize, but she was requiring him to tell her every name he was known by, as there might only be one of his names she recognized.

The spirit of the man refused to turn around and face her so that Dancing Wind could clearly see his hands and face. With his back turned towards her, he angrily told her, *"YOU NEVER TRUSTED ME."*

Dancing Wind felt the danger this spirit represented, so she angrily replied: "IT IS WITH DAMN GOOD REASON I NEVER TRUSTED YOU!" Then Dancing Wind told him, "NOW TURN AROUND AND FACE ME

SO I CAN SEE ALL OF YOU CLEARLY, AND TELL ME ALL OF YOUR NAMES!"

But this the treacherous spirit would not do, so Dancing Wind promptly reinforced her White Light of Protection and returned to the Indian village with Dan. As evening approached, they climbed down off the mountain making it to their cars just as the sun was setting in the western sky.

Back home, they talked about the day's events. Dancing Wind said, "I know the Spanish death traps that were placed on the mountain centuries ago were there to decoy anyone looking for the Spanish gold away from the cache site where it had been placed. Yet Lily, I thought you were taking me to a treasure."

"I did guide you towards a treasure. To me, the spiritual treasures are most important."

"Were I, or any other Guardian Angel, to look over this entire mesa, all would agree I took you as close as I could to a priceless spiritual treasure."

"I know you wanted a treasure of Spanish gold or silver but first you need to be able to recognize danger and learn how to deal with it."

Dan said, "Did you notice that once on top of the mesa, Lily had taken over leading you to the Indian village? She knew that the evil spirit was there and he would try and lure you to his killing ground."

Lily said, "I was keeping up a steady conversation with you so that I knew you were paying close attention to what I said in case the situation turned deadly. I wanted you to become aware of the terrible things this man has done so you would understand the help his victims needed.

Dan then added, "We wanted you to gain experience encountering a evil spirit while both Lily and I were here to intercede if our help was needed. We both realized you needed this experience so as to ensure your success, when in the future you encounter them again, or when both of us are not around."

"Lily was giving you "hints" such as, *'Why is the spirit keeping his back to you? Would not a friendly spirit come up and introduce himself? Is he acting like a friend?'* For these are the very questions you must ask yourself when you encounter another spirit. You must always realize a friendly and honorable spirit will show it in his actions and deeds."

Lily told Dancing Wind, "This spirit intended to kill you, as he has often killed many women and children! If you are up to it I would like you to take the spirits of the women and children he has murdered *home.*"

Dan added, "You have obviously encountered this evil man before, in a past life, as he said to you: 'YOU NEVER TRUSTED ME.' This evil spirit was a man who throughout his previous life liked to kill women and kids. He has done so many times. He was trying to lure you to his killing ground so when you witness his evil behavior he was hoping you would drop your White Light of Protection so he could attack you."

Lily told Dancing Wind, "The real treasure that I want you to take off Mesa de Abiquiu is the poor lost earthbound spirits that the evil man had raped and murdered. It is time for the women and kids to let go of the fear, the hurt, the outrage and suffering and return *home* to GOD. The loved ones of the murdered women and children who missed them so much are anxiously awaiting their return *home.* These spirits have been badly hurt and they needed lots of prayers and love.'

"When you are ready, if we work together, we can take them home. It is too dangerous for you to go to his killing ground as he has the home field advantage. Your White Light of Protection may be difficult for you to hold firmly in place when you witness how he has hurt so many spirits. Let me know when you are ready and a group of us (Angles) will gather them up and escort them down to the bosque and we will all work together to taking them back to their loved ones."

What these spirits of the women and children really needed was a miracle! What they got was a teenage Arapaho Indian girl just learning how to track trails in the realm of the spirit!

****

Late in the fall of that year, when winter was close at hand, the candles and prayer fire were lit. Down by the Chama River, in the Bosque (the wooded area along the river) beside the tall cottonwoods a young Arapaho girl called on the Great Spirit for help. She called upon the Great Spirit to send his Angels for help to take the women and children *home.*

Beside the Chama River, her prayer fire burned as she played the flute. She would pause occasionally to add wood to the fire and warm her fingers. The air was cold, and she sat upon the frozen ground of Mother Earth. At times she would be lost in the flute music she played. Occasionally she paused in playing her music to converse with one of the spirits that arrived to join her, or listen to the Angels giving her guidance. In the distance she heard some ducks flying south. Twice she thought she heard an owl call.

Sometimes she gave her full attention to one of the women or children's spirits who needed an extra word of comfort, a special prayer, or just a hug. Tears ran down the teenager's face at the tragic and senseless murders she witnessed in one- to three-second flashes that several of the spirits showed her. But she was happy too, as she also experienced the relief and gratitude many spirits expressed to her for helping them to break free. She smiled as she knew that finally they would be going *home.*

Dancing Wind called in all the spirits who in love and light, chose to go *home* now. All the women and children who had been murdered southeast of the Indian village had come to go *home.* Other Spirits she did not know had also tagged along as they wanted to go *home,* too! Dancing Wind welcomed them all to join her in love and light at the sacred fire. Then near the burning fire, two Angels appeared one on each side of the door of light.

The Spirits formed a line at Dancing Wind's request and one by one passed through a door of light. They were going *home, home* to the Great Spirit! Dancing Wind said one last goodbye to each spirit as they paused before the Tunnel of Light. The two Angels standing guard entered the tunnel; and as suddenly as the Tunnel of Light appeared, it was gone. As the fire burned low, the tears ran down Dancing Wind's cheeks and she cried and cried.

Note from the Author

I would love to hear from my readers. While I may not be able to answer all my correspondence you can be sure I will read all your letters. Should you wish to receive an e-mail of new books as they are published, you can write me and send me your e-mail address.

Anyone who wishes to receive a free short story of Dancing Wind's adventures can receive it via e-mail for the asking. The readers will need to be patient with me as it may take several months to answer your request as I may be out in the field tracking trails with my good friend Dan and Dancing Hawk.

I have written four books with stories of Dancing Wind and her friends. They are available on Amazon, and also as a Kindle E-story, and their delivery time will be weeks faster than mine. If you like my stories, please tell your friends or, better yet, give them your favorite book as a gift.

Barton Thom
trackingwithangels@yahoo.com
Dancing Hawk Press, 223 East Maxan St. # 107
Port Isabel, Texas 78578

Tracking with Angels
Flight of the Angels
Path of the Angels
Justice of the Angels

Each book is $19.95, and I will pay the postage in the United States.

Please remember, Amazon and Kindle ship promptly. I take about two months at my Port Isabel, Texas address. Yet, if time allows, I will try and answer your letter.

GOD SPEED,

Barton

www.ingramcontent.com/pod-product-compliance
Lightning Source LLC
Chambersburg PA
CBHW060253100426
42742CB00011B/1734